The Parables of Jesus

THE PARABLES OF JESUS

Recovering the Art of Listening

Richard Q. Ford

FORTRESS PRESS
MINNEAPOLIS

THE PARABLES OF JESUS
Recovering the Art of Listening

Book and cover design by Joseph Bonyata.
Cover art: *Der Zwölfjährige Jesus,* Albert Paris Gütersloh, 1937. Copyright © 1997 Artists Rights Society (ARS), New York / VBK, Vienna. Used by permission.
Author photo: Virginia K. Ford

Readers wishing to comment on this work may contact the author at Box 222, Williamstown, MA 01267 or by e-mail at richard.q.ford@worldnet.att.net

Library of Congress Cataloging-in-Publication Data

Ford, Richard Q.
The parables of Jesus : recovering the art of listening / Richard
Q. Ford
   p.   cm.
Includes bibliographical references and indexes.
ISBN 0-8006-2938-8 (alk. paper)
1. Jesus Christ—Parables. I. Title
BT375.2.F67 1997
226.8'06—dc21   97-29607
                                         CIP

Manufactured in the U.S.A.   1-2938

01   00   99   98   97   1   2   3   4   5   6   7   8   9   10

For Karen and John

May your ongoing explorations
of the biblical tradition
be as exciting and rewarding as my own

Contents

Introduction

Others will object that my expositions are overly subtle, that Jesus'
parables are simple stories for simple people. Such is the arrogance
of us moderns that we fail to recognize true complexity when it
appears to us in unfamiliar forms.

—Bernard Brandon Scott

Interpretation does not make anything clearer; rather, it offers
another level of meaning.

—Edgar A. Levenson

Probing the parables of Jesus may be described as the opportunity and
work of each generation of persons attracted to the biblical tradition.[1]
This book addresses those engaged by Jesus' discourse who suspect
unexplored aspects in his parables and who want resources on how to
proceed. It is written by a clinical psychologist long interested in
responding to these brief, enigmatic stories with the particular ways of
listening practiced by psychotherapists.

I have chosen to focus on seven of the longer parables, those usually
titled the Dishonest Steward, the Talents, the Unforgiving Servant, the
Unjust Judge, the Wicked Tenants, the Prodigal Son, and the Vineyard
Workers.

Modern scholars generally agree that the basic outlines of these stories, though not necessarily their exact words, originate with the historical Jesus. Their common themes and shared structures persuade me that
all are the product of a single, masterful imagination.[2]

In terms of common themes, each narrative presents two persons, or
groups of persons, in conflict. One side is stronger and in control; the

other is weaker and obliged to comply. Yet each partner in these unbalanced twosomes wants something from the other. The economically stronger of the two hopes to entrust to his subordinate something he values.[3] In the midst of being controlled, the subordinate attempts to respond. These efforts at collaboration are stretched across wide social, economic, and, in one case each, generational and gender differences.[4]

All seven stories also share a common structure made up of three scenes. The first describes the superior engaging his subordinate both to entrust what he values and to impose what he believes. The second discloses how the subordinate, left alone, replies to this combination of entrusting and control. In the third, the superior returns to pass judgment on the subordinate's choice.

I have taken these narratives out of their later contexts in the Gospels in order to study them together as a group.[5] Making comparisons across all seven steadies one's hand when reaching to discern the extraordinary ambiguities compressed within their narrow spaces.

This book differs from most written about these parables; its difference arises from the kind of work I do. In listening to these stories, I use ways in which psychotherapists have been trained to listen.[6]

Therapists invite, respect, and struggle with the distortions that regularly occur when two persons of different backgrounds try to stay together, when they want something from each other, and when at least one of them resists either controlling or being controlled.

Therapists assume that all of us, in our efforts to achieve safety and to remain comfortable, exclude from awareness parts of our experience. Believing that what is excluded contributes to what ails us, therapists try to hear what is missing.[7] Thus, they listen for how clients (as well as they themselves) are inattentive, blur distinctions, and assume the perspectives of others to be the same as their own. They also listen for how clients (as well as they themselves) look for others who seem different, place in those others attributes of their own that they fear, do not notice this transfer, and then use the resulting contrast as evidence of weakness in the other and strength in themselves.

When bringing such concepts into contact with these parables, I have come to believe that in each story the two main characters are misunderstanding one another. I will propose that each is trying to make the other fit preconceived expectations, that is, each is attempting to avoid anxiety by distorting who the other person is. This effort at control, understandably, is met by the other's resistance.

Using my experience of the misunderstandings that take place between client and therapist, I explore possible analogues between (1) the mutual misperceptions that may occur between the two main parable characters, and (2) the misperceptions that may engage a listener who is trying to understand a parable.

Throughout this book I will be inviting readers to evaluate at least three areas of potential misunderstanding, three ways in which parable listeners may be tempted to reduce complexity by excluding information.

Idealizing the Superior Character

The first area of possible misunderstanding involves a too-ready acceptance of the contexts provided for these parables in the New Testament. (Two of these stories are found in Matthew alone, three in Luke alone, one has versions in Matthew and Luke, and one has versions in all three Synoptic Gospels as well as the Gospel of Thomas.) Scholars have long understood that the particular perspectives of the editors of these Gospels determined both where they placed their inherited materials as well as how they revised what had been handed down to them in order better to serve their own points of view,[8] Listeners across the centuries have been aided and impeded by the specific literary contexts in which these editors, writing perhaps forty to seventy years after Jesus taught, chose to situate what originally had been oft-spoken narratives.

I will argue that in the process of establishing their own immensely creative perspectives, the Gospel editors understood these parables in ways that have tended to unsettle carefully crafted balances essential to their functioning. With few exceptions,[9] modern interpreters have followed these editors in ascribing any untoward developments in each story wholly to the economically weaker of its two participants. So persuaded, they embrace at face value the apparent negative qualities of each less-powerful protagonist; they see as fully explanatory the subordinate's overcaution, ungratefulness, dishonesty, profligacy, or murderousness.

Such denigrations of the subordinate occur because these same Gospel editors regularly assume that the economically superior figure represents some aspect of divine intent. Thus, the dishonest manager's tolerant employer, the unforgiving slave's forgiving slave-master, the generous vineyard owner and the trusting vineyard owner, the slave-master supplying the silver talents, and the forgiving father of the prodigal son are each construed by the Gospel editors as a figure for God. (The unjust judge is seen as a complete opposite.) Listeners are thus drawn to elevate the positive qualities of the more powerful figure into an uncomplicated predominance. That character, for example, is seen as straightforwardly generous, forgiving, or incisive.

In such understandings, the economically superior character acts in surprising ways to overturn the expectations of the listener: a rich man commends his dishonest estate manager; an assertive slave-master commends autonomy and condemns passivity; a compassionate slave-master releases his debtor slave; a law-abiding landlord seeks recognition from rebellious tenant farmers; a loving father forgives his profligate son; and a generous landowner pays unanticipated wages.

By agreeing with the Gospel editors to establish the economically powerful character as a figure for God, listeners tend to construct black and white patterns of inclusion and exclusion. The superior becomes the source of all resolution while the subordinate remains the repository of all difficulty; the more powerful is revered and the weaker is shouldered with the blame. This bias, steadfastly resisting all evidence of weakness in the superior and strength in the subordinate, has endured for twenty centuries.

Yet if Jesus is the creator of these parables, if his attitude is aptly caught in the aphorism, "Blessed are the destitute," and if there is historical accuracy in accounts of his presence among social outcasts, then it would be curious indeed if his imagination excluded representations of God ever from being found among the economically oppressed, preferring instead to locate that presence exclusively among the powerful.

This process of perceiving one person in a twosome as the source of all of the solutions—and none of the problems—is termed, in psychotherapy, "idealization." Openly, the one idealizing locates most of the available competence in the admired other; secretly, the person who idealizes is trying to hand over to someone else all the difficult work.

This common deception can be further understood as part of a process known as "projection." In this process unacceptable impulses in oneself are placed outward onto others, who are then rejected, while the individual's conscious sense of self remains identified with those idealized others who are perceived as all good. One gains power by being like—and liked by—the one who has the power.

For psychotherapists, the problems and opportunities of being idealized are a daily fare. Wishing to avoid painful, risky work, clients regularly ascribe to their therapists the ability to set things right.

The temptation to idealize—and for the other to believe in the idealization—may be found in ready example in the Prodigal Son. Here the elder son may be seen as preventing himself from becoming his own person through persisting in the exhausting and exhausted hope that his father will provide that status for him. His claim on his father for recognition of his own competencies, once necessary but now beyond realization, remains both the unrewarded focus of his energies and the continuing refuge from his risks. And the father does not help him. He both frustrates his son's desire for recognition and fails to recognize his son's need for autonomy. The father is aware of what he, the father, provides but not of what his son independently produces. If the listener, following the Gospel editor Luke, idealizes the father as a figure for God, he joins the son in mistakenly locating within the father all of the resources for the son's growth.

When approaching these parables, one is free to go in either of at least two directions: (1) to follow the Gospel editors and perceive in the superior character's actions and attitudes some representation of divine intention—a position that supplies all of the pivotal definitions from within the superior's point of view, or (2) to perceive a balanced and complex tension between two persons, with each contributing to the evident pain of their compromised interdependence.

This second option calls upon listeners to resist segregating the two major characters into exclusive categories of restorative and destructive. I will propose that listeners may equally well perceive both characters as together involved in a developing drama in which the actions of one intimately affect the responses of the other. Neither is simply correct; neither is simply wrong.

The chapters in this book are representative of this second approach; I find that it leads to a balanced, steadily unsteady tension both within the narrative and between narrative and listener. I hope to demonstrate that these seven parables can be understood in both directions.[10] The choice—and the awareness of choosing—then falls to the listener.

Collapsing Parable Time

A second area of potential misunderstanding concerns the amount of time one allows for these stories to unfold. Because they are generally understood to refer only to a single point, listeners often hear them quickly and quickly dismiss them as known; as a corollary, they usually assume their time span to be brief.

Yet longstanding realities may be compressed within their narrow compass. As each parable opens, the two main characters have for their lifetimes been captive to those legalized conventions of antiquity that segregated individuals into rigid social roles—such as landed aristocrat, slave-master, estate manager, widow, peasant, tenant farmer, day laborer, and slave. Thus, the true beginnings of these stories may be as distant as the origins of those entrenched social roles endemic to the ancient imperialisms that invaded Israel at least since the time of Alexander the Great.

Although the social and economic distances separating them are huge, the parable protagonists take a momentous step: they attempt to collaborate. These efforts, in turn, enliven the enduring but usually dormant realities of their massive differences. Propelled into potential awareness are longstanding dilemmas otherwise blurred in the seeming normalcy of everyday living. Using the span of a day, or of weeks, or of months, these parables arouse—but never make explicit—the effects of decades and even centuries of institutionalized control. Thus, for modern listeners, extensive amounts of time may need to be imagined—both before these narratives begin and from within the large absences of description located throughout their telling.

For example, in the Talents, when the last slave, instead of investing it, buries his master's entrusted money, listeners are tempted to join the slave-master in misperceiving the slave's irritating timidity as if it were simply the result of current weakness. It may be, however, that the slave is communicating as immediate passivity his outrage at a lifetime of being enslaved. Neither slave-master nor parable listener may readily suspect the disguised but effective resources of those endlessly dominated to frustrate the initiatives of those endlessly domineering. We, like the slave-master, are tempted to perceive only the immediate symptoms of resistance and not the distant evidences of betrayal. We, as he, may further our ignorance by isolating events from their beginnings—as if the present fact of being timid has nothing at all to do with the ancient fact of being enslaved.

Therapists learn to study sequence, that is, to wonder, Before this happened, what happened? Across the broad sweep of a person's development, therapists assume that current distortions were originally born of fear, and that what is now out of awareness was at some point not able to be tolerated. Such exclusions, in turn, are not simply the fault of any individual child or parent. Rather they survive as evidence of those aberrant emotional forces that march down through the generations and into the histories of us all.

Parable time may feel foreshortened for a second reason: these stories are quickly told. Their brevity is the product of an oral culture. Jesus, as far as we know, did not read or write, nor did he communicate with many who did. His parables were meant to be spoken, heard, and remembered; as a consequence, they are brief. Modern readers, however, are tempted to move rapidly across their compressed sequences. They lack the experience of an attentive, illiterate listener who is permitted, without the intrusion of other competing words, to ponder their unfolding over long periods of time. Especially are modern readers liable to miss a crucial component of the parable form, namely, how much, not being said, is carefully committed to the listener's imagination.

The brevity of each story, necessary to an oral culture, may function as a screen. The listener, indeed, is allowed to accept the apparent short space of time as all there is and move on. But if one pushes backwards into the story, delays, and attends to the nature of time, she or he can, I believe, discover accounts of remarkable subtlety, imbued with irony, that bring the hearer to a place of disconcerting wonder.

Ignoring What Does Not Make Sense

By extending the amount of time enclosed in these narratives, one will arrive, I think, at an increased awareness of details in each story that make no ready sense. Probing these anomalies reveals a third area of potential listener misunderstanding; it involves a too-early relinquishing of sustained curiosity.

The past three decades of parable interpretation in North America have seen increased challenges to the idea that the parables have a single point or even several points—or, put another way, that they can be reduced to ideas able to be stated in sentences.

Replacing this understanding is the view that these narratives evoke in the listener efforts to integrate into a coherent whole the parable's surprising developments. Such efforts can be expressed in prose only partially and with difficulty. With this new understanding, inquiry into the vicissitudes of listener response has become a major area for discovery in contemporary parable research.[11]

Scott, following Iser, observes that these parables require the listener to create out of their disparate parts some kind of consistency. Yet the consistency usually sought involves integrating the surprising or generous initiatives of the superior character. As did Crossan before him, Scott emphasizes how these initiatives "shatter" a prior consistency confidently anticipated by the listener.[12]

Focusing the attention of listeners on such "shattering" highlights the initiatives of the superior character and what the parable does with the listener. Such a strategy tends to establish the superior as someone able to effect substantial change without having first to hear and understand his subordinate's experience. By contrast, I am going to encourage listeners to attend to the great amount of distorted interaction that has occurred between two unequal persons before the narrative begins and to what the listener does with the details in each story that make no sense.

For example, in the Dishonest Steward, why would an astute and capable estate manager, wholly dependent on his employer's goodwill to escape expulsion into the class of expendable day laborers, carelessly squander that goodwill? In the Talents, why does the third slave, openly fearful of his master's demanding greed, not do immediately as his master later prescribes and invest the troublesome money with bankers? In the Unforgiving Servant, why would an obviously competent slave, calculating enough to garner a huge loan, be stupid enough to cashier an insignificant colleague in easy view of his recently compassionate lord?

In the Unjust Judge, why does a person so denigrating of tradition and so disinterested in other people insist on occupying one of the few positions in society that requires both profound respect for tradition and the constant intrusion of others? In the Wicked Tenants, why would a father, who possesses abundant evidence that his distant tenant farmers are violently opposed to him, propel his own son into their midst unprotected? In the Prodigal Son, what does the father intend when he violates the norms of every culture in every era in order to transmit to his children control over his assets while he is still alive? And in the Vineyard Workers, what is the landowner attempting when he provides a transient generosity to a group of day laborers he otherwise consistently deprives?

I will notice throughout how listeners make many and differing choices when trying to render coherent these incoherent details. In my experience, the scope of listener choice expands markedly when sustained attention is paid to the ways in which important details of these stories do not, in fact, cohere.

The Work of Parable Listening

When describing the work of parable listening, I will be entertaining the hypothesis that the parable functions, in relation to a listener, the way a therapist functions in relation to a client. Both relationships—parable and listener, therapist and client—offer stably unstable processes in which new experience may be created through difficult collaboration between two connected but unequal participants. Like a therapist, the parable presents skillfully unexplained gaps or silences into which the listener is lured to supply her or his own expectations.

Paralleling the misperceptions that occur between parable characters, paralleled in turn by the misunderstandings that take place between client and therapist, may be the distortions listeners encounter within themselves when attempting to discover meaning in each story. I hope to demonstrate repeatedly that each stage in what the parable does depends intimately on what choices the listener earlier makes. Here the listener may share the position of both parable protagonist and client: each engages in the study of studied ambiguity. Here the parable may be understood as providing, as does a therapist, a many-sided, tentative receptacle for the listener's enduring expectations. These expectations the parable steadily returns to us for our evaluation.

For example, when listening, do you tend to take sides? Do you question the actions of the superior figure as closely as you do those of the subordinate? Within one character's experience, do you stay on one side of his or her ambivalence or try to keep in balance both sides? Do you attempt to reach closure by discarding differences? Do you entertain, in spite of the superior character's final pronouncements, the possibility that true resolution has yet to occur, and that what has been achieved thus far may be merely the continuation of misunderstanding in an even more disguised form?

Comprehending these enigmatic stories of Jesus may well involve us in wondering about the very ways we choose to comprehend.

1

A Manager and a Rich Man

Of the parables attributed to Jesus, the Dishonest Steward is widely held to be among the most difficult to understand. Some of the difficulty arises because of uncertainty about the financial and contractual relationships involved. But for most listeners the story is troubling because it appears to condone dishonesty. The narrative reads as follows:

The Situation
There was a rich man who had a manager,

Scene I
and charges were brought to him that this man was squandering his property. So he summoned him and said to him, "What is this that I hear about you? Give me an accounting of your management, because you cannot be my manager any longer."

Scene II
Then the manager said to himself, "What will I do, now that my master is taking the position away from me? I am not strong enough to dig, and I am ashamed to beg. I have decided what to do so that, when I am dismissed as manager, people may welcome me into their homes." So, summoning his master's debtors one by one, he asked the first, "How much do you owe my master?" He answered, "A hundred jugs of olive oil." He said to him, "Take your bill, sit down quickly, and make it fifty." Then he asked another, "And how much do you owe?" He replied, "A hundred

containers of wheat." He said to him, "Take your bill and make it eighty."

Scene III
And his master commended the dishonest manager because he had acted shrewdly. (Luke 16:1b-8a)[1]

Two ancient conventions are presumed in this story: (1) The manager is trusted by master and debtors alike to enter into contracts on the master's behalf and with the master's authority. Should the manager prove incompetent or criminal, the master is obligated publicly to revoke that authority. (2) The debtors owe the master money in the form of promissory notes, written by themselves, to be honored at the time of harvest. Substantial amounts of money are at stake: the oil has a value of about three years' wages for the average worker at that time; the wheat is worth the equivalent of a wage earner's income for about seven and a half years.[2]

Writers on this parable, here renamed more neutrally A Manager and a Rich Man, almost always divide its two main characters into separate compartments, usually labeled "bad" and "good." The actions of one seem to have little to do with the actions of the other. The manager is often perceived as clever, dishonest, and a rogue. The rich man, by contrast, is generally understood as acting within his rights, and, at the end, given unexpectedly to praise. The impact of the story is usually located in one of two places: listeners are to emulate the later decisiveness (not the dishonesty) of the manager, or one's expectations are overturned by the master's surprising commendation.

What Makes the Manager Squander?

This man was squandering [his master's] property. . . . His master commended the . . . manager because he had acted shrewdly. . . .

One place to begin in this difficult story is with an improbable contrast rarely noticed as such. At the end of the narrative the manager has acted, in the Greek, *phronimos*, that is, shrewdly, sensibly, thoughtfully, prudently, wisely; yet at the beginning he is introduced as reckless.

As the story opens, the manager is described as wasting or squandering his master's property. This same Greek verb, *diaskorpidzo*, appears in two other of our parables: in the Prodigal Son, where the younger son squanders his inheritance, and in the Talents, where the slave-master has the reputation of a hard man who gathers where he has not scattered seed. The verb's basic idea is of scattering, as in the scattering of seed or in the dispersing of a flock of sheep. It connotes an absence of precision in planning or an inability to control an outcome. The parable describes the manager as squandering the rich man's property, not stealing it. Stealing implies both calculation and greed. Squandering, by contrast, suggests either revenge or depression; the verb remains ambiguous as to whether the manager intends to waste or has become helplessly imprecise.

In either case, this very same person is soon to be presented as shrewd, wise, and sensible. In this way the parable juxtaposes incompatible qualities: careless squandering that ignores self-interest and clever, calculating action wholly devoted to self-interest. How does this man move from a position of carelessness to one of shrewdness? How can one locate these opposing attitudes coherently within the ongoing processes of the same person?

Many listeners ascribe this change to the man's suddenly losing his job. Caught in an emergency, the manager jumps to attention. Well enough. But the later qualities he so swiftly manifests must have been present all along. A more revealing question might be, How in the first place did the manager lose control of his shrewd abilities?

The listener is led backwards into the story. What happened before the manager began his squandering? How did he arrive at this place of scattered and scattering behavior where altogether absent are his earlier and later competencies?

Certainly when authorizing him to conduct negotiations on his behalf and announcing him as such to the surrounding business community, the rich man had believed both in his manager's honesty and in his competence. Listeners learn that for some time the manager had in fact exercised that competency, binding his master through numerous, valuable contracts.

Then, however, the manager inexplicably changes. He is no longer competent. He loses focus. He withdraws from the energetic oversight of his responsibilities. He becomes careless and even mindless. What has happened?

The manager is not likely to be a chronic incompetent, able for a time to mask his inability. What then would one make of the person who vested him with authority in the first place? Would this man of wealth be impoverished in discerning precisely those qualities requisite for the management of that wealth? That the rich man accurately estimated his subordinate's abilities is evident in the manager's early and later skill. However one construes the master's final praise, no one is left in doubt about the manager's reconstituted astuteness.

Nor will it do at this point to emphasize the manager's dishonesty. Were he dishonest, he would now be stealing, not squandering. But here he has no stomach for the calculation that embezzlement requires. The issue at this stage is not criminality; it is carelessness. The listener is left to wonder how this capable person became aimless and indifferent. No rational goal can be discerned in his squandering; he appears to be out of control. What could have happened?

The Listener's Contribution

Here is a major gap in the narrative. With this masterful and nearly seamless presentation of ambiguity, the parable, like a toll collector at a bridge, now demands something. To move on, the listener must select one from among a number of possible causes to account for the manager's shift from shrewdness to thoughtlessness.[3] As listeners we cannot avoid such contributing; we can only not notice we are doing it.[4]

The most popular listener choice at this juncture is also among the most mindless, that is, lacking in explanatory power: the manager is assumed to have a prior disposition to dishonesty; somehow he has always been a rogue. At the very least such listeners have confused squandering with dishonesty.

I suggest instead that the manager, who reveals himself as a dependent person reliant on both the recognition and the risk-taking capacities of others, has lost the centerpiece of his self-confidence; he has been deprived of his master's responsive support. I assume that the manager is rendered careless because he has become depressed; I further assume he has become depressed because he has been neglected.

Later on I will argue that these assumptions give coherence to many of the puzzling details of this story. But my hope at this crossroads in listening is not so much to advance this particular decision as to highlight the fact of listener contribution. In agreeing or disagreeing with my choice, you may be better able to observe the one you are making. Whatever option you select—and you must decide something—will have a profound effect on your understanding of the rest of the parable.

To aid in exploring this narrative further, I want at this point to introduce some of the ways psychotherapists learn to listen.

Some Resources from Psychotherapy

One large convention in these stories that is often assumed but not often examined is the intermingling of differences in social status with forms of intimacy and trust. In literal terms, the more powerful person entrusts the use of his wealth or status to someone less powerful. In analogous terms, one now enters the sphere of any human relationship in which power is unevenly distributed but trust is sought: women and men, employers and employees, therapists and clients, teachers and students, parents and children, even mothers and infants. One person in a twosome possesses more, knows more, controls more but wishes to give some of what she or he has into the hands of someone who possesses less, knows less, or controls less.

What happens when someone who dominates another also wants to trust that other? What happens when the person dominated also wants to trust the one more powerful?

The person less powerful will respond within or against the conventions of obedience but also in terms of being trusted. Reactions of complying or refusing to comply to the use of force are less complex than the range of potential responses to trust and its breakdown. Within this larger and freer space of belief in another may be discovered themes of longing, betrayal, love, envy, hope, and disillusionment (to name a few), depending on what happens in the communication of trust across inequality.

The British psychoanalyst D. W. Winnicott proposes that one cannot understand an individual in isolation. We can only know someone in terms of her or his relation to a particular other person, especially those with power who come into the range of trust. We most often believe in ourselves in direct response to how such trusted others believe in us.

Emotional symptoms—distorted speech, inappropriate feelings, and troubling actions—are not themselves the difficulty. Just as individuals cannot be comprehended without knowing how significant others have responded to them, so symptoms do not exist in isolation. Instead, emotional symptoms come into being as disguised signifiers of attempts to remain in contact with trusted others who have, for important reasons, become untrustworthy.[5]

In this context of an emotional symptom as a hidden but potentially intelligible communication, Winnicott offers specific theorizing about the meaning of some antisocial behaviors in children. His comments have a direct bearing on the present parable. Winnicott suggests that an antisocial act can at times be an expression of hope:

> I was asked by a friend to discuss the case of her son, the eldest of a family of four. She could not bring John to me in an open way because of her husband, who objects to psychology on religious grounds. All she could do was to have a talk with me about the boy's compulsion to steal, which was developing into something quite serious; he was stealing in a big way from shops as well as at home. It was not possible for practical reasons to arrange for anything else but for the mother and myself to have a quick meal at a restaurant, in the course of which she told me about the troubles and asked me for advice. There was nothing for me to do unless I could do it then and there. . . .
>
> I said: "Why not tell him that you know that when he steals he is not wanting the things that he steals but he is looking for something that he has a right to; that he is making a claim on his mother and father because he feels deprived of their love." . . . I may say that I knew enough of this family, in which both the parents are musicians, to see how it was that this boy had become to some extent a deprived child, although he has a good home.[6]

This interpretation, communicated through the mother to her son, resulted in the son's stopping his stealing, here understood as an ending of the son's need to speak in a disguised fashion. The message hidden within the symptom was finally grasped.

Part of the symptom's disguise is found in its malevolence. Because the antisocial act appears as an attack rather than an effort to communicate, the sender has not risked as much as he would had he made a direct appeal. Anything more straightforward would be too vulnerable to humiliation were it to be met with the anticipated rejection.

A further component of the antisocial act, in Winnicott's understanding, is that it compels the person addressed to attend. Neither the sender nor the receiver of the masked message is aware of this intent, but the action has the great value of breaking through a growing barrier made up of inattention in one person and a corresponding withdrawal by the other. In this sense the antisocial act is an act of hope. It is a last-ditch effort to communicate that something good and positive has existed but that such goodness is being lost. The person is attempting to say, "I steal in order to tell you, in the safest way available, that you, from whom I need giving, are stealing from me."

The Manager's Inability to Speak

Returning to the parable, we are enabled to ask the following questions. What may be disguised in the manager's symptom of thoughtless scattering? What is communicated but not yet understood? In particular, what may have happened between master and manager to make this symptom intelligible?[7]

Three major clues, at least, point to possible answers. As a first clue, we learn that the manager is preoccupied with being dependent; his single-minded objective is to keep hold of his position. Deeply concerned with his own security, he repeats in his soliloquy the pronouns "I" and "me":

> *Then the manager said to himself: "What will **I** do, now that my master is taking the position away from **me**? **I** am not strong enough to dig, and **I** am ashamed to beg. **I** have decided what to do so that, when **I** am dismissed as manager, people may welcome **me** into their homes."*

This dependent manager reaches out to be enveloped by the larger capacities of others. He hopes to act "so that people may welcome me into their homes." He is a person, in short, who is preoccupied with being protected.

He has good reason to be so concerned. Within the social and economic conventions of Mediterranean antiquity, he is enmeshed in a client-patron relationship that renders him wholly reliant on his patron's whim. Herzog describes the manager's position as follows:

> A retainer in the household of an elite was nearly as dependent as a slave, but without the security associated with slavery. . . . If the steward loses his position, he loses not just a stewardship but access to the household bureaucracy itself. . . . To lose his stewardship and join the work force of day laborers is to drop out of the retainer class into the class of expendables.[8]

If one infers from the substantial value of the commodities bound under contract, the manager is collaborating with his aristocratic employer to increase the latter's wealth at the expense of less wealthy farmers. Those preyed upon are likely to be the natural enemies of both men. Thus, the manager is dependent on his lord not only for his position but also for his protection.

Beyond these economic and social realities may also lie others more personal. To establish these, it is first necessary to notice the rich man's reciprocal dependency. As an absentee landlord, this aristocrat relies on his manager to secure the wealth he must have if he is to defend his own position. Herzog describes the rich man's counter-dependency.

> It has taken years of work to learn what it takes to succeed as a steward. [The manager thus] represents an investment to the master, who needs trustworthy stewards to keep his estates productive and profitable so that he can pursue an active role in the constant struggle with other elites and with the ruler.[9]

At a personal level, then, the heightened suspicion endemic to almost every other relationship available to either man would render particularly gratifying the trust essential to their collaboration. These two isolated co-conspirators are in some ways tied together as father and son—or as a godfather and his lieutenant. Each requires the other in order to function.

Because such intense interdependency is found in a context largely devoid of other resources for security, this manager, I believe, has to be highly sensitive to any hint of breakdown in his master's trust.

The Rich Man's Inability to Hear

A second clue to the reasons for the manager's squandering lies in the master's difficulty in discerning that symptom as a communication hoping for a response.

At the beginning of the narrative the master has succeeded for some time in not knowing that his manager is wasting his goods. Others learn of the squandering, and some eventually tell the rich man, but he himself remains ignorant. Here is a triangle: two who know (the manager and those who bring charges) and one who does not (the master). How the master's ignorance comes about is not revealed, but somehow, in a relationship requiring mutual awareness, vacancies in that awareness have arisen:

> *There was a rich man who had a manager, and charges were brought to him that this man was squandering his property. So he summoned him and said to him, "What is this I hear about you? Give me an accounting of your management, because you cannot be my manager any longer."*

When the accusation finally lands in his lap, the master fails again, this time openly, to become curious about what ails his employee. Given the importance of his subordinate's position, the manager's instant dismissal is understandable. When the rich man hears rumors of untrustworthiness, he acts first and finds out what happened later.

Nevertheless, one would expect that someone with so much of his own trust betrayed would be aroused to discover the source of his subordinate's attack. Why does the rich man not go on to demand the reasons for his subordinate's breach of trust? How is it he makes no inquiry at all?

Some have supposed that the manager's lack of self-defense corroborates his guilt. His silence in the face of accusation, however, might also reflect despair at his master's failure to become at all concerned, or at least curious, about him.

The master's inability to inquire into the manager's reasons for the squandering, and the manager's inability to articulate those same reasons to his lord, are remarkable. Each has lost his capacity to speak openly to the other. The silence, at this point in the narrative, is deafening. The manager's soliloquy and subsequent actions altogether miss the mark. The true target, the master, has disappeared. In what had been an open relationship of some trust, silence has so overtaken speech that even the reasons for the speechlessness are now buried in graves without markers.

Putting these two clues together, I suggest that what this dependent manager has lost, and what renders him unable to function, is his certainty that his master thinks well of him. At the point when the manager begins to sense that he may be losing his patron's regard—and well before he has to confront the fact of losing his position—he begins to feel depleted of a resource essential to his competence.[10] Losing the sure knowledge of his master's confidence, he in turn loses confidence in himself. Since neither person is able to speak to the other about the real problem, the manager fills the emptiness with the speech of silence, that is, with a symptom. He becomes depressed, and within his depression, careless.

He squanders his master's property; he scatters it with no concern about getting it back. Stealing, in fact, would have expressed more hope. There the message would be, "I am trying to get back what I once had." Squandering, by contrast, suggests hopelessness. In a convoluted way the manager may be attempting to say, "Whether you let go of me or didn't, I feel the loss of your regard. I feel hurt and hopeless. So I am doing to you what I believe you have done to me. I let go of what belongs to you because I believe you have so let go of me."

I postulate, then, the manager's perception of a loss of interest in him by his master—a perception this dependent person cannot tolerate. Unable to feel his master's ongoing recognition, the manager falls into a depressed collapse. He squanders in order to represent in a precise but disguised manner what he experiences his master as having done with him. His scattering of goods is in response to his master's scattering of care.

The rich man, in turn, is unable to discern in the hurtful act the hidden message of appeal.

We mark the mid-point of an intimate tragedy. At this stage the reader, influenced both by the parable's Gospel context and a long-standing interpretive tradition, which idealizes the master, may be feeling increasingly restless. But a crucial, third clue supporting this line of approach is at once more evident and more difficult to discern. Its significance is almost universally ignored.

> *So [the rich man] summoned [his manager] and said to him, "... you cannot be my manager any longer." Then the manager said to himself, "... my master is taking the position away from me. ... I have decided what to do so that, when I am dismissed as manager. ...."*

This clue, twice repeated, is muted in the text. It is first found inside the manager's rumination, "since my master *is taking* the position away from me. ..." As the manager walks down the hall to get the accounting books, he has indeed been dismissed by his employer; however, as far as the debtors know, he is still in office.

The parable offers a second chance to become aware of the rich man's surprising failure publicly to curtail his subordinate's authority. Not only does the manager observe that his dismissal has not yet been accomplished, he repeats that fact ("... so that *when* I am dismissed as manager. ...").

The manager's ability to summon and command his master's wealthy debtors, each of whom owes tens of thousands of dollars, depends entirely on the latter's belief that the manager remains vested with his master's authority. Clearly the debtors would not have risked altering their contracts if they could not assume—as they had correctly up to that moment—that the manager was acting with the consent of his employer. Had the man of wealth at once informed these important debtors of the dismissal, the latter could not possibly have colluded with the manager, thereby imperiling the source of their needed loans.[11]

But the rich man fails to notify his debtors; the manager's message to them outreaches that of his lord. Breech finds it commendable that the rich man, following the interview, continues to believe that his manager will turn in a true account of his management.[12] Yet more is at stake at this moment than an accounting. The man of wealth, by failing at once publicly to disavow his failed manager's authority, colludes in tempting into danger an entire business community dependent on the rich man's goodwill. When contemplating the manager's subsequent dishonesty, listeners tend to hold his master in no way responsible. Nonetheless, in spite of having just judged him as incompetent or dishonest or both, the rich man continues to lend authority to his squandering agent. How is he, immediately after discharging him, unable to recognize that he is still allowing his employee control not only over his assets but over his public reputation as well?

Entertaining this question may involve a prior suspicion that the master has already contributed to the untoward actions of his subordinate. Earlier on, I assume, the master did not recognize his squandering manager's need for his presence, for his active inquiry, and perhaps for his discipline. The master's attention is elsewhere than on his manager; the manager's attention, in consequence, is elsewhere than on his master's property. Only a third party, the unnamed bearer(s) of the charges, notices and acts on both lapses. Without this outside intervention, one suspects that these two might have colluded in their mutual avoidance for some time to come.

Supplied with reports that his manager is squandering his goods, the rich man responds, but in a way that facilitates his manager's further squandering. The humiliation the rich man here permits exceeds the harm he has until now been forced to accept. Who at this point is responsible? The manager, who continues to behave with a faithlessness others have already described? Or the master, who persists—this time fully informed—in failing to control his out-of- control subordinate?[13]

This moment is central to the story. Until now the manager is not dishonest. At this point, however, both persons are in trouble. Whatever the master is about, he has by his inaction acted recklessly.

The Manager's Despair

Following the master's inadequate response to the manager's inadequate behavior, the latter changes dramatically. He abruptly ceases to act in a thoughtless and scattered manner; instead he skillfully begins to plan. He is now with utmost calculation paying out his master's property for specific and urgent ends. His attention is knotted to the breaking point. What has caused him to change?

It is easy to imagine the manager's anger at being reproached; harder to suppose may be his despair at being ignored. The manager must now comprehend two conflicting messages, neither of which addresses his underlying distress: his abrupt dismissal without inquiry and his continuation in authority without control. Earlier, before the squandering, the manager felt his master ignoring him. Then he felt ignored again by the master's failure to inquire into—not the charges—but the meaning of his behavior. Now, finally, he is once more ignored by the inexplicable act of allowing him continued access to power.

All the while, important words describing what is happening are absent. The rich man has not spoken to the true issue. He has failed to perceive what the squandering was about. Now, in relaxing his authoritative control, what can the master mean? Can he be signaling anything other than a lapse in valuing not only his manager's integrity but also his own? In response, the manager shifts his desire away from his unreachable, collapsing lord and toward other potential masters.

A question begins to focus. Does the manager decide to betray simply on his own, or is he responding both to his master's previous ignoring of his squandering now coupled with an even more inexplicable failure immediately to close him down?

It may not matter whether the manager's character is upright or corrupt. As he walks down the hall to get the books, the (upright-leaning) manager may feel shamed by his master's inability to get beyond the charges and discern the muddled longings disguised within his untoward behavior. In despair, he may feel compelled to continue, but now in a more focused and convoluted manner, his distorted efforts to communicate his desire for inclusion. On the other hand, the (corrupt-leaning) manager may experience himself as loosed of needed control and enticed by the master's inability to rein in his damaging impulses. He may feel seduced, even, by the rich man's implicit permission to steal. (The manager is not here exonerated; the point is, rather, that he is not acting in a vacuum.)

Listeners may imagine at this juncture that the manager has more options open to him than the one he chooses. Many suppose he remains free to return to straightforward discourse with his lord well before the master himself becomes able to ask, "Why has my competent manager squandered my goods?"

Yet is such an expectation reasonable? Should the subordinate be first to risk dialogue without his superior at least hinting that he may also be responsible? It is difficult to suspect the manager's loss of hope when he inchoately realizes, given his master's ongoing silence, that he may at this point have no other choice than to become more corrupt.

Has the manager in fact any option open to him other than to proceed further with the unraveling, to keep going toward collapse, in a desperate effort to make the master understand? In this context of increasing nonrecognition, the manager's response may be limited to an even more disguised symptom: carelessness will now be replaced by dishonesty; such dishonesty may be among the few remaining actions available to represent the unhindered escalation of misunderstanding on both sides. .

This entire sequence is now loaded into a single representation of the whole. It is this impoverished representation (the manager's dishonesty), and not the larger history of their relating (the unarticulated and unacknowledged progression of misunderstanding between the two protagonists), that so commands the listener's attention. By making illegal provision to the debtors, the manager hopes to compensate for his loss of recognition from his lord. Ironically, it is this heavily disguised symptom—and not his earlier competencies and incompetencies—that at last elicits the longed-for recognition.

In the master's commendation the manager does indeed evoke a form of recognition. But precisely because he was reduced to coercing it, the praise the manager finally receives becomes a mockery of that for which he had so much hoped. And the cost to him in the end will be far greater than he ever imagined.

The four Greek words here translated as "dishonest manager," *ton oikonomon tais adikias,* form what is termed a "genitive of quality," that is, the combining with a noun of an attribute (in noun form) that ordinarily would be provided by an adjective.[14] Thus, these words may be translated literally as "the manager of unrighteousness," or, even more literally, "the manager of the not right."

Proposed at this level of literalness, two questions may now be formed: What in this story is not right? And is the manager able to manage it?

The crime earning the manager the description "dishonest" and taking up so much of the parable's space, both misleads the listener and defeats the manager. His actions mislead because, in this reading, his behavior represents a symptom of something else. His actions defeat because in the end they will fail to realize the security he seeks.

The manager's crime cannot possibly provide him such security. Not only, in his urgency, is he unconcerned about the harm he is doing to his master; he is also, despite his shrewdness, unaware of the damage he is doing to himself. He is in fact calculating his safety in ways that only increase his danger. After twice squandering his master's goods, he proceeds to squander his own future.

For he is erecting his external dishonesty upon an internal deception. He persuades himself that he will secure the trust of new masters through the betrayal of old. Yet these new masters will not mistake his intent upon their colleague. The debtors may for a time pay him off with favors; none, however, will be taken in by taking him in. Who among them would entrust the management of his wealth to someone so prepared to betray?[15]

The debtors have no access to the private distress underlying the public betrayal. As most of us do much of the time, they see only the immediate evidences of the betrayal itself. The manager will be welcomed, of course, but in the end certainly discarded.

For all his prudent efforts, this person has succeeded merely in imposing on his future a pattern forced on him by his past. He is able to reproduce only what has so wounded him already: he will excite the active interest of others while ensuring their ultimate neglect. Just as his own longing for the concern of a stronger man was betrayed, so he, by betrayal, will influence other stronger men most surely to betray him.

The Rich Man's Bind

Both debtors and lookers-on alike can have no access to the true source of the master's commendation. The rich man leaves his debtors, depending on how one reads the latter's inclinations, either in a kind of ethical limbo or in a moment of unusual opportunity. They may suspect the manager's tenuous position, since its basis is already known to those who bring the charges. They may even anticipate the master's imminent discipline. But since the rich man has not yet told them of his decision, the debtors remain free to accept his beneficence as administered by his manager. Who are they to turn down such lucrative offers? Are they not, in spite of their suspicions or even certain private knowledge, still free to rationalize their good fortune either by assuming the rich man's generosity or, as is more likely, by realizing that a puzzling misjudgment has left him wide open to their taking advantage?

The debtors perceive that the rich man will have no choice but to act the part of a generous landlord. They calculate he will be forced to ratify his manager's action. To recant would be to acknowledge his own stupidity in continuing in authority someone already known to be out of control. With feelings ranging between sadness and delight, the debtors understand that by commending his rogue manager the rich man is covering up his own incompetence.[16]

The latter's praise, full of silence, is replete with irony. Beyond the awareness of all but perhaps the betrayed manager, the master must now speak falsely because earlier he failed to speak. With his few commending words, he frees himself from many honest words. Appearing generous, he avoids his own humiliation. Throughout the entire sequence he has been unable to hear what his manager, first dismissed from awareness, then dismissed in shame, and now dismissed with praise, has all along been trying to say.

As the community of his debtors and neighbors looks on with some combination of embarrassment, anxiety, and pleasure, the rich man now stands secretly shamed. He may not suspect his own participation; he may feel simply misused. But if he senses his own contribution, with what kind of regret, anger, and longing may he now be experiencing his missed opportunities?

If the two had been able to explore in words the private hurt of each, how might they have been able to avoid these larger hurts, nurtured in silence, covered over with praise, and now flowing unimpeded into self-defeating consequences?

Listening in Ways a Therapist Listens

Psychotherapists work in the arena of anxiety, that is, where the expectation of danger leads to varied expressions of assault and to varied evidences of flight. By attempting to transform subjective distress into curiosity, they hope to widen the opportunity for both therapist and client to make discoveries. I want here to indicate how a listener might hear a parable using the steps a therapist attempts when listening to a client.

First, as the client begins to trust the therapist, he reveals characteristic ways of expressing anxiety, for example, by attacking, blaming, enticing, or withdrawing. The therapist tries not to react but instead to stay present and remain curious.

Next, if all goes well, the therapist begins to discover recreated within herself some version of those conflicts and even terrors the client has long known. At times the therapist may be tempted to act on some part of that version. More often she feels the seeming impossibility of any resolution. Thus, enclosed inside the client's world, the therapist resists acting and instead struggles within herself first to name what she is experiencing (for example, her wish to attack the client and her fear of destroying him) and from there to suppose what the client might be experiencing (for example, his wish to attack the therapist and his fear of destroying her). She is aided in her work by the hypothesis that the feelings the client is engendering in her were originally engendered in the client. The therapist's curiosity facilitates an environment in which the client may risk new ways of speaking.

Third, the therapist is aware of the necessity of an open-ended, tolerant, steady presence to permit this building up of new experience. These conditions of safety—the therapist's taking in of difficult feelings and then developing an attitude of wondering—are not won all at once; they emerge slowly and are complicated by many upsets along the way.

Such steps in therapist listening may provide analogues for parable listening. When entering the parable, the listener encounters tension between its two main participants. Something difficult to describe is motivating their puzzling behaviors. The listener feels pressured to resolve these tensions. The most readily available responses are the same as the most common responses to anxiety, namely, some form of fight or flight. Fight involves taking sides and blaming; flight involves a decision to stop paying attention. The listener's task may be to do neither, but instead to remain within this area of bewildering tension and to become curious.

Therapists are trained to assume that what the client now does to the therapist is a version of what in the past was done to the client. Using this assumption, the parable listener may suppose that the confusion and distress the parable produces in the listener is a version of the confusion and distress experienced by the characters themselves.

Let us return to the question of what the astute manager is trying to accomplish by defrauding the rich man. The usual response is that by ingratiating himself with his master's wealthy debtors he is seeking future security. Such certainly is his conscious intent. Yet, if you place yourself in the position of those debtors, would you be likely to entrust the management of your wealth to someone who has already revealed a capacity to defraud? It would appear that the manager, in the very act of trying to achieve it, is in fact further endangering his future security.

It is precisely at this moment of confusion that a therapist is trained to become curious. She will approach her own bewilderment with the confidence that she has become privileged to experience the manager's anxiety-engendered confusion—and now has the chance to wrestle within herself to make some sense of it. She assumes (1) that her inner state arises from within the manager's world, and (2) that the reasons for it are disguised. She then persists in trying to remain inside that world and to attend especially to those portions of it that make little sense.

The therapist may then do the following work and arrive at the following hypotheses:

1. The therapist observes, "This person is trying to make me trust him by ingratiating himself with me by fraudulent means. He thinks he is enhancing my confidence in him but in fact he is doing the opposite. His behavior makes me trust him less, not more. I notice that I want to get away from him."

2. Rather than acting on this impulse and emotionally withdrawing from the manager—as would happen in most social situations—the therapist instead becomes curious: "What could possibly be happening that this person is making me want to do the opposite (reject him) of what he says he wants me to do (take him in, give him a home)?"

3. The therapist now consults this feeling aroused in her of wanting to withdraw from the manager. Once again, she is aided by the prevalent hypothesis among psychotherapists that what the client is doing to her (making her want to withdraw from him) is likely to be a version of what some important figure in his past has done to him.

4. The therapist might then suppose the following sequence, here reported in backwards order: (a) the manager is trying to buy my interest in him in a way that makes me want to withdraw from him; (b) that may mean he does not trust me to want him simply for his own abilities;

(c) that may mean he has come to doubt his own abilities; (d) however, he used to have considerable self-confidence. What can have happened?

5. The therapist might then hypothesize, "Could it be that what this person is now doing to me is a representation of what also has happened to him? Could it be that he is experiencing the effects of someone who has stopped wanting him for his own abilities, some important other who has withdrawn from him?"

In sum, one way a therapist understands what the client may have experienced in the past is to consult what experience in the present the client is evoking inside her.

We may extrapolate this strategy for parable listening. From the array of differing responses the parable evokes within us, we begin to assemble a collage of conflicting feelings and attitudes. As in a progressing psychotherapy, we may then entertain the possibility that what the manager is doing to us has been done to him, and that the manager's confusing behavior is part of a two-person field. Put another way, the listener's confusion about the manager's behavior occurs because probable contributions to it by the master have until now been excluded from awareness.[17]

An Invitation to Decide

It may be that this parable (along with the others in this book) offers no conclusive definitions of how to be or what to do. It may resist providing meanings by which one may measure oneself. This restraint, this refusal to define, may be the result of presenting two disparate but balanced versions of reality.

The parable listener may be invited toward a stance similar to that of a therapist, toward an overlapping and even simultaneous hearing of two very different but perhaps equally valid points of view.

In my work as a psychotherapist, I have learned that certain kinds of therapist silence, certain withholdings of understanding, can be the product of true caring. Such restraint is not well described by the popular concept of the therapist's unresponsiveness. It rather represents the therapist's efforts to create a situation in which the client may tell his own story in his own way, on his own terms, and in his own time, yet within a structure able to contain and tolerate his necessary anxiety.

In a context of unfolding safety, the therapist carefully limits responding in ways that the client has learned both to expect and to evoke. In the slowly expanding space between what the client expects and what the therapist does not do, unnoticed and therefore troubling parts of the client's experience are gradually allowed, felt, expressed, observed, and named.

Necessary here is the therapist's ability to empathize simultaneously with ambivalent parts of the client's dilemmas. She resists taking sides, does not become an advocate, but rather holds in tension multiple possibilities. She tries to be present while at the same time aware of unexpressed, contrasting feelings. She knows that in the world of the client what is happening at the moment is not all of what is happening; always lying in wait is the other side of the client's ambivalence.

The same two-sided uncertainty, the same balancing of disparate points of view within a context of carefully crafted gaps or silences, may also be characteristic of a parable's unfolding. And the only one able to recognize the resulting misperceptions and to bridge the gulf between the two parable protagonists may be the listener. She or he alone may be positioned to penetrate the inarticulate misunderstandings of both sides, be in touch with each, comprehend their differences, and imagine what both might have to do in order to bring about some resolution.[18] Here the listener is the one who completes the story. Here the familiar separation between an author who gives and an audience that receives may be breached.[19]

These two interrelated ideas—the possibility that the parables offer no conclusive answers and that their resolutions may instead be entrusted to listeners—are likely to be resisted by many readers. We tend to accept life as justly hierarchical. We want someone from above to provide us with authoritative interpretations.[20] A college student once asked, altogether perplexed, "If Jesus knew what the kingdom of God was, why didn't he just say so?"

Apart from wanting answers to the question, "Well, what does the parable mean?" readers may be responding that I have been piling assumption upon assumption. I want to notice and underscore this critique; I believe it to be an unavoidable fact of parable interpreting. For at each place that I have been called upon to introduce an explanation, so have you. It is my hope that for every assumption you observe me making, you may become aware of one of your own.

The listener's perception that the rich man wastes his own goods, squanders his manager, and scatters the confidence of the surrounding business community becomes available only as a possibility enclosed within an earlier possibility. This lack in the master, contributing to the final tragedy, is open to surmise only if the listener does not fill in the original gap between the two protagonists by immediately taking sides with the rich man against the manager.

The parable seems in its design to lure the listener to such a taking of sides. The evidence for the original breakdown of trust is muted. The later, malevolent consequence of the entire sequence, the manager's dishonesty, is magnified. If the listener opts for this proffered path of taking sides, then the possibility of the master's collusion in the tragedy, which can become obvious, instead becomes obscure.

The manager exhibits no awareness of, nor guilt about, the possibility that he is in any way responsible for the destruction of the rich man's trust.[21] Yet, it is the listener alone who must decide where in the sequence of events this accurate observation falls. Is the manager's failure of concern for his lord prior to or consequent upon the master's failure of concern for his manager? How is the second's concern for the well-being of the first related to the first's concern for the well-being of the second?

As you try to understand a parable, your choices of where to enter and where to leave its sequence become, I believe, two of your most important decisions.

2

Three Slaves and a Master

Usually titled the Talents or the Pounds, this parable confronts the listener with a strange moment in the world of masters and slaves.[1] The behavior of its major character, a timid slave, makes no sense. He knows well that his master insists on taking in what he does not deposit and on reaping where he does not sow; fully aware of these harsh expectations, this seemingly fearful subordinate proceeds—unnecessarily—both to frustrate his master and to humiliate himself. When confronting his lord's demand to get something for nothing, this last slave, in marked contrast to his fellows, does nothing at all.

The parable has two versions,[2] here presented side by side:

The Situation

For it is as if a man, going on a journey, summoned his slaves	*He summoned ten of his slaves,*

Scene 1

and entrusted his property to them; to one he gave five talents, to another two, to another one, to each according to his ability. Then he went away.	*and gave them ten pounds, and said to them, "Do business with these until I come back."*

Scene 2

The one who had received the five talents went off at once and traded with them, and made five more talents. In the same way the one who had the two talents made two more talents. But the one who had received the one talent went off and dug a hole in the ground and hid his master's money.

Scene 3

After a long time the master of those slaves came and settled accounts with them. Then the one who had received the five talents came forward, bringing five more talents, saying, "Master you handed over to me five talents; see, I have made five more talents." His master said to him, "Well done, good and trustworthy slave; you have been trustworthy in a few things. I will put you in charge of many things. . . ." And the one with the two talents also came forward, saying, "Master, you handed over to me two talents; see, I have made two more talents." His master

When he returned . . . he ordered these slaves, to whom he had given the money, to be summoned so that he might find out what they had gained by trading. The first came forward and said, "Lord, your pound has made ten more pounds." He said to him, "Well done, good slave! Because you have been trustworthy in a very small thing, take charge. . . ." Then the second came, saying, "Lord, your pound has made five pounds." He said to him, "And you. . . ."

said to him, "Well done, good and trustworthy slave; you have been trustworthy in a few things. I will put you in charge of many things. . . ."

Then the one who had received the one talent also came forward, saying, "Master, I knew that you were a harsh man, reaping where you did not sow, and gathering where you did not scatter seed; so I was afraid, and I went and hid your talent in the ground. Here you have what is yours."

Then the other came, saying, "Lord, here is your pound. I wrapped it up in a piece of cloth, for I was afraid of you, because you are a harsh man; you take what you did not deposit, and reap what you did not sow."

But his master replied, "You wicked and lazy slave! You knew, did you, that I reap where I did not sow, and gather where I did not sow? Then you ought to have invested my money with the bankers, and on my return I would have received what was my own with interest. So take the talent from him, and give it to the one with the ten talents." (Matthew 25:14–21b, 22–23b, 24–28)

He said to him, "I will judge you by your own words, you wicked slave! You knew, did you, that I was a harsh man, taking what I did not deposit and reaping what I did not sow? Why then did you not put my money into the bank? Then when I returned, I could have collected it with interest." He said to the bystanders, "Take the pound from him and give it to the one who has ten pounds." (Luke 19:13, 15-24)[3]

This parable suffers from a pervasive misperception, the consequence of an unfortunate collusion between modern Western values, and the altogether different motives of the Gospel editors of Matthew and Luke. Taken together, however, these perspectives imbue the story's exacting master both with integrity and with the consequent authority accurately to evaluate his well-positioned slaves. In the judgment of nearly every contemporary First World commentator, this dominant parable protagonist is someone to be believed.

Only Western listeners, steeped in the mores of modern capitalism, could so thoroughly miss what was obvious to Jesus' original peasant audiences, namely, that this master's mode of operating is criminal. Herzog, Fortna, Rohrbaugh, and Kahler are among the very few First World observers to grasp this fact. Herzog, using the work of Cardenal, writes that of "all the contemporary commentators on the parable, the peasants of Solentiname were the ones to intuit the economic system that underlies the parable [as] . . . 'a very ugly example . . . of exploitation.'" Fortna, building on the insight of an unnamed, underclass prison inmate, describes the master as engaged in aploitative enterprise." Rohrbaugh, understanding that in the closed agrarian economy of peasant Galilee "a larger share for one automatically means a smaller share for someone else," suggests that in such a world "a master getting one thousand per cent on his money would be viewed as greedy to the core." Kahler is more explicit; he sees the master as "inhumanly hard," "a blood-sucker," "an oppressor," "a thief," "a usurer," and "a loan-shark."[4]

Having farmed out to trusted lieutenants both capital and entrepreneurial risk, this absentee master is realizing profits of between 100 and 1,000 percent. The last slave clearly describes the nature of his enterprise: "You [are] a harsh man, reaping where you did not sow, and gathering where you did not scatter seed. . . ."

Yet modern Western listeners have great difficulty perceiving the viciousness inherent in this man's behavior. Part of this difficulty lies in the manifest pleasure of the collaborating exploiters. But much of it lies in their stringent refusal to acknowledge their victims.

When asymmetry in power exists between two groups over a long period of time, the more powerful will try to transform the subjective experience of those less powerful. Dominant persons have an immense interest in how their right to control is defined; invariably they justify their dominance by imposing self-serving rationalizations on those less able to fight back. The stronger will press their versions of reality into the weaker—and then, with equal tenacity, will resist experiencing the painful consequences of what they themselves have imposed.[5]

Evidence of such self-serving rationalizing is found in the language both used and not used by the first slave when reporting his "success":

> "Lord, your pound has made [from the Greek *prosergadzomai*, to make more, earn in addition] ten more pounds." (Luke 19:16)

> "Master . . . , I have made [from the Greek *kerdaino*, to gain] five more talents." (Matthew 25:20)

Neither does the pound make more pounds nor does the slave gain more talents. Absent is any reference to the essential work of peasant farmers, day laborers, artisans, and slaves—all of whom this powerful slave has robbed in order to create the obscene profits he presents to his lord. [6] The parable may thus be perceived to have three levels, two of which are explicit and one that is not:

(1) the exploiting slave-master
(2) the well-positioned slaves who are called upon to exploit
(3) the poorly positioned laborers who are exploited

Contemplating these three levels, one begins to realize how aptly they capture the economic realities in the Galilee of Jesus' era, where all such activity was rigidly segregated into three tiers:

(1) distant Roman overlords, rapacious of their colonies, who masked their greed under a facade of law
(2) coopted Jewish aristocrats, endlessly taxing and otherwise exploiting their fellow Jews, who kept some of the siphoned-off wealth for themselves but surrendered much of it to Rome
(3) hapless, unrecognized, victimized laborers—peasants, artisans, slaves—who were the sole producers for the Empire

The Exploited Called Upon to Exploit

To understand this parable, we need to understand these three groups, starting with the distant overlords.

In the Roman Room of the Boston Museum of Fine Arts stands a series of busts, highly realistic and deriving from the late Republic and early Empire. One has only to look into the faces of these people—clear-sighted, intelligent, but with the most intense, steel-eyed determination—to realize why they ruled the world.

The minuscule governing class of the Roman Empire relentlessly extracted wealth from its vast pool of laborers. Through innumerable patronage webs these overlords collected and then redistributed that wealth first among themselves and then to the small surrounding retainer classes of bureaucrats, landowners, and soldiers. The orientation of these ruling groups was hierarchical, authoritarian, exploitative, and punitive.[7]

The vast majority of the populace—peasants, artisans, slaves, and hangers-on—was illiterate, marginally nourished, voiceless, devoid of any ability to organize, and positioned indefinitely to be exploited. The orientation of this great majority was to be "wantless," that is, to be insulated as far as possible from exploitation.

Carney summarizes the overall situation as follows:

> The economic surpluses produced by these traditional preindustrial societies were meager. Hence there was little to go around, and that little was inadequate for the elites, with their lifestyles of conspicuous consumption. Consequently, the lower orders lived near starvation level, and the resources of their betters constantly fell short of their "needs."[8]

Absent from this society—and thus unable to act as an ameliorating counter-force between the exploiting minority and the exploited majority—was anything resembling a modern middle class. No third group stood between the rapacious extractor and the resourceless oppressed. The ideologies of patron and master held sway, unchecked, under the guise of law.

Here appears that particular grouping of interdependent but irreconcilable attitudes essential to a society of oppressors and oppressed. The

landed Jewish aristocrats of Jesus' time, whom I propose may be represented by the parable's well-positioned slaves, were caught right in the middle.

During the period in which Jesus lived (ca. 6 B.C.E. to ca. 30 C.E.),[9]
Galilee was part of a client kingdom in the hinterlands of the Roman
Empire. It knew the wider *Pax Romana* achieved under Augustus and
continued under Tiberius, together with the narrower peace maintained
in Galilee by its puppet ruler, the Tetrarch Herod Antipas (3 B.C.E. to 39
C.E.). This world was one of stable, if massive, political and economic
inequity. Jesus was not responding, as would the later Gospel editors, to
the terror of an aroused Roman revenge that led in 70 C.E. to the rav-
aging of Jerusalem and the consequent collapse of religious and political
stability. He was living, rather, within the rationalized subtleties of
peaceful, everyday exploitation.

Overtaxing of the peasantry, including the obligatory Temple tax, was
a major form of such exploitation, but one overtaken by the aristocracy's
insidious expropriation of peasant land. Through exorbitant loans and
inevitable foreclosures, the elites forced increasing numbers of peasants
off their ancestral lands and into the class of expendable day laborers.
The gradual development in first-century Galilee of a market economy,
with the substitution of cash crops in place of bartering, only increased
the rate at which wealth was transferred from the peasants to the urban
elite. The rebuilding, in Galilee, of Sepphoris and the later building of
the new capital, Tiberias, further served to drain immense resources
from the surrounding countryside.[10]

It is not generally recognized that although Jesus spent most of his life
in a Jewish peasant village of about 150 persons (Nazareth), he grew up
within four miles of Sepphoris, the largest city in Galilee, boasting a population of somewhat less than 10,000. Sepphoris was the terminus of the
north-south road from Jerusalem. It was also positioned along one of the
busiest east-west trade routes of ancient Palestine, placing it in ready
commerce with the rest of the Empire. A major center for the region's
Jewish aristocracy, its leading families were directly beholden to its
Herodian ruler, who in turn was directly beholden to Rome.[11]

During the reign of Herod the Great (40 B.C.E. to 4 B.C.E.), "Sepphoris became his principal fortress town from which to rule and tax
Galilee."[12] Josephus reports that, following Herod's death in 4 B.C.E., "a
large number of desperate men at Sepphoris . . . made an assault on the
royal fortress/palace, and made off with all the goods that had been

seized there."[13] Rome reacted with brutal ferocity; the surrounding villages were devastated and their inhabitants enslaved. Herod's successor, the Tetrarch Herod Antipas, made Sepphoris his provincial capital from about 3 B.C.E. to about 18 C.E. At least some archaeological evidence appears to confirm Josephus' report that Antipas had the city rebuilt.[14]

Meier concludes that "Jesus . . . was born—most likely in Nazareth, not Bethlehem, ca. 7 or 6 B.C. . . . "[15] Thus, the disastrous rebellion initiated by the peasants surrounding Sepphoris would have occurred during Jesus' early childhood and Sepphoris itself rebuilt, at the expense of peasant resources, during his later childhood and adolescence.

Himself an artisan whose family was without land, Jesus is described as a *tekton* (Mark 6:3), probably meaning a "worker in wood."[16] Since Sepphoris was the area's major population center and a little over an hour's walk away, it seems reasonable to suppose that Jesus at times worked for the elite Jews of Sepphoris.[17] (By this proposition I mean to imply not that he imbibed their values but merely that he observed their dilemmas.)

Several pieces of evidence from the late 60s C.E. hint at the dual tensions facing the Jewish aristocracy of Sepphoris. The first, indicating collusion with their Roman overlords, was the unusual decision of the city fathers in 69 C.E. to strike coins bearing the name of the Roman General Vespasian. Meshorer cites this numismatic evidence as confirmation of Josephus' report that of all the cities in Galilee, Sepphoris in the late 60s C.E. was alone in supporting Rome.[18] The second, concerning their relations with the surrounding peasantry is that the Galilean peasants, in this same period just before the war, pillaged portions of Sepphoris.[19]

I am assuming that analogous tensions between subservience to Rome and loyalty to their own religious heritage strained the Jewish aristocracy of Sepphoris during the time of Jesus. I do so primarily because of Jesus' selection for this parable of the metaphor "slave." For years I had been puzzled why a devout Jew living within Israel would be attracted to such an image. As metaphor, "slave" implies the gradual overwhelming of all resistance, with the resultant incorporation of the conqueror's ideology. Those so controlled eventually surrender to mere compliance; imaginative opposition ceases. "Slave" has overtones of the well-nigh irresistible penetration of one person's identity into the life workings of another.[20]

Now this is not a metaphor applicable in Roman occupied Palestine to either Jewish pharisee or Jewish peasant. Neither, whatever the force

of the outsider's power, was ever tempted to incorporate that alien's ideology. One group, however, was. One group had begun to relinquish the
far more egalitarian understandings of land distribution and debt allevi-
ation inherent in the values of ancient Israel. One group, by agreeing to
exploit, had begun to incorporate the values of their exploiters. "Slave"
might well serve as metaphor for the insidious erosions of integrity
threatening those Jewish elites thriving, through subservience to Rome,
in the Hellenized cities of Galilee.

The Gospel editors report that during his teaching and healing in
Galilee Jesus avoided these cities. Considering this slave parable, however, it is not so clear that Jesus avoided pondering the particular issues
deeply affecting their compromised Jewish elites.[21] What happens, for
example, when you attempt to move from the integrity of traditional
Nazareth to the conflicting currents of cosmopolitan Sepphoris? What
happens when you step outside of tradition and instead reach for elements of the same power that has already coerced your own compliance?
What happens if you then begin to identify with your captors and start
to agree that their modes of exploitation may be lawful, that is, reflective
of reality? Such a temptation is present for peoples of any time when
their traditional values are pressed hard by the values of an alien power.
One is pulled, in the jargon of psychoanalysis, to "identify with the
aggressor," that is, to try to master the experience of being oppressed by
becoming a smaller version of the oppressor.

With this background we may be better positioned to struggle with
the puzzling response of the present parable's main character. Timid as
he is, this last slave is the only one in the story who does not exploit.
Located somewhere between overlord and peasant, he is neither liberated
nor quisling.

The Last Slave's Impotence

> Then the one who had received the one talent also came forward, say-
> ing, "Master, I knew that you were a harsh man, reaping where you
> did not sow, and gathering where you did not scatter seed; so I was
> afraid, and I went and hid your talent in the ground. Here you have
> what is yours." But his master replied, "You wicked and lazy slave!"

The last slave's conflicting perspectives produce the major tension in this story. On the one hand, he claims to be afraid of his master, whom he knows to be demanding of unearned profits; on the other hand, he refuses to invest. Moreover, he seems unaware of the danger inherent in his passivity; during his report he betrays no concern that he might be provoking his master's anger. Whether innocently or as a result of depression or with disguised skill, this slave simply offers as fact his failure, inability, or refusal to take action.

On first examination, the last slave's decision to hide the money seems puzzling indeed. He says that he is afraid; his fear suggests that he wants to protect himself from being punished. Yet if he grasps, as he claims he does, his master's harsh expectations, how could he be so unthinking? His master wants to collect interest. The slave wants to avoid recrimination. Obviously his safest course is to invest the money. He need not be, as his fellows were, stunningly successful; he had merely to take a minor risk. Should he then fail, he would still be safe. The master spells it out for him: "You ought to have invested my money with the bankers."

In the final scene the slave is almost insulting.[22] "I knew you were a harsh man, reaping where you did not sow . . . so . . . I went and hid your talent in the ground." At this blatant nonsequitur the master, understandably, becomes furious. The last slave could hardly have found a more effective way to offend this particular master. No option available to him was better calculated to incur the displeasure of such an intensely aggrandizing aristocrat than doing nothing at all. By refusing risk, he redoubles his risk.

The story thus poses this question: How could such a cautious, apparently fearful slave, both in his act of hiding and in his self-justifying speech, so badly miscalculate what to do in order to be safe? The reasons behind this seeming miscalculation, not being provided, must be supposed.

The listener is here presented with a major gap, or unexplained sequence, in the parable. This sequence is made up of three parts, no one of which fits well with the other two:

1. The slave says he is afraid of his master.
2. The slave does the opposite of what he knows his master wants.
3. The slave tells his master (a) that he is afraid of him, and (b) that he did not do what he knew his master wanted, without acknowledging that (a) and (b) do not fit together.

How differently the parable would read if, in the final scene, the slave either claimed ignorance of his master's desire or else showed feelings of anxiety or remorse. It is difficult to suppose which behavior offended the master more: the slave's hiding the money or his acting as if knowledge of what his lord wanted in no way affected his decision.

These three disjointed parts can be integrated by at least two different explanations. The story can function using either.

In a first understanding, the slave is by character unaware. He in fact does not comprehend what he claims to know of his master's intent. Instead he acts consistently with his constricted style. Although he can describe the difference between himself (fearful) and his master (harsh), he nonetheless firmly believes, given his nose-to-the-ground, avoidant perspective, that his master wants the single response that he, the slave, is able to imagine. He is convinced his best service is to keep the money unproductively safe. His conservative act innocently but firmly frustrates his superior's desire. When confronted with his master's anger, he is surprised. "I did what you wanted," he says. "I kept what belongs to you safe."[23]

In an alternate understanding, this particular slave, unlike his fellows, is unprepared for independent initiative. He knows very well what his master wants but he cannot do it. So he shuts down. He puts the money in a safe place and refuses to think about it. When the master finally appears, the slave is forced to describe the dilemma he could not solve. Some sentences from Winnicott might apply here: "A child who has reached a certain degree of personality organization meets with an experience such that it is beyond his power to deal with it. . . . The management of . . . [such] phenomena . . . presents so great a difficulty that the child puts [himself under] . . . comprehensive control—with depressive mood as the clinical result." In Winnicott's terms, the slave can conceive of no way out other than to stop functioning; he becomes depressed.[24]

The Master's Disappointment

"You are a harsh man; you take what you did not deposit, and reap what you did not sow."

The master is secure in his aristocratic assumptions. He betrays the unexamined confidence of someone entitled to consume without having to imagine the feelings of those compelled to produce. "I deserve," he insists, "something for nothing." Now, however, instead of exercising his power directly, he invites his slaves to imitate him. In thus trying to entrust across difference, he arrives at a boundary he may not always be able to cross. For he has here chosen to shift from demanding a subservience he can require to wanting an imitation he must evoke. To be able to entice such mimicry—at least with some of his slaves—he may in fact be obliged first to acknowledge a contradiction he cannot even see, namely, that he wants his slaves to act as he does but not become as he is. He remains unaware of the irony inherent in his effort to foster mastery while still remaining master. (That a number of his slaves seem unimpressed by such a conflict further distracts the listener from supposing that it might exist.)

Described earlier were two possible ways the last slave might have experienced the offer to take initiative. What follows are parallel descriptions suggesting how this same slave might earlier have responded inwardly to these unacknowledged, contradictory attitudes in his lord.

In the first reading, the master's efforts at communication are completely stymied. The lord has no power at all to break through this particular slave's inability to register the former's invitation to greed. The slave has found a way, entirely outside his awareness, to erase his master's desire with a ferocity and completeness fully equal to the manner in which his master has all along erased him.

An alternate understanding emphasizes not denial but helplessness. Because he has been so totally dominated, the last slave has developed almost no identity of his own. He exists largely as the product of his master's definitions. Yet at the very moment he is invited to make decisions, he loses the master who has always made those decisions for him. This slave lacks what the master has blocked him from developing, namely, the capacity for independent initiative. Put differently, this particular slave embodies but half of his master's ambivalence: the capacity to comply as a slave but not the capacity to decide as a master. "The last slave could not become a full investor in his own eyes largely because the original investor, the master, refused to acknowledge him as anything other than an investment."[25]

In both these readings the master participates in his own disappointment. The last slave fails either because he is unreachable or because he is traumatized into inaction. In either case the lord receives a response shaped by his own prior assumptions, a major one being that he does not, in his effort to encourage their independence, have to take into account the prior effects of his dominance.

These readings are ironic. With his last slave, the master confronts a contradiction and its denial. This subordinate tells him, "I knew what you wanted, and yet I hid your money. I do not even now acknowledge the contradiction in what I am saying." Yet the master may also, within himself, be refusing to recognize a prior contradiction. "I want you to act as a master, and yet I want you to remain a slave. I do not even now acknowledge the contradiction in what I am saying." If the master, in this matter of changing others, has obligations he has yet to embrace, then considerable irony also resides in the last slave's description of his character: "You are a harsh man," he observes. "You reap what you did not sow."

Although many listeners disapprove of the last slave's apparent assumption that the master wants the same response that he, the slave, chooses to give, these same listeners often accept a parallel assumption of the master, namely, that the slave should want the same response that he, the master, chooses to expect. Even more, many listeners seem ready to agree that masters indeed have not only the right but also the ability to compel other persons, however incapable or unprepared, to conform to their desires.

The Last Slave's Potency

The one who had received the one talent went off and dug a hole in the ground and hid his master's money.

There may be a third way to comprehend the behavior of the last slave. He may be superbly calculating. Within the constraints of his position, he may be engaged in a carefully disguised attack upon his lord's presumption. Under cover of a cowering facade, he has in fact undertaken a calculated rejection. Citing fear as his motive, he is refusing to exploit. He will resist imposing upon others what has been perpetrated upon himself. The listener becomes increasingly aware that this apparently passive person may be far from weak. It is as if the slave is saying, with a skillfully crafted indirection, "I will be hard on a hard man by being soft."[26]

Here one might conceive a battle between equals, distorted by inequality. That the master selects this slave for trial indicates the former's estimate of his potential. But the lord may have mistaken as aptitude for raw power a more complex determination to retain dignity. When the test comes, this slave neither exploits nor steals. By refusing, he counters every effort of his master to dominate him; by doing nothing, he engages in a courageous effort to maintain his integrity.

In this reading, the last slave is as alert as his lord to wrest something from nothing. His seeming passivity is, of course, a dangerous activity. He is fully aware that he will provoke his master's censure and that beyond humiliation and immediate punishment lies the risk of further enslavement. During his lord's long absence he may well have experienced an ongoing tension between the demands of the system and the pressures of his conscience. He may well have been tempted, many times, to invest with the bankers.

Integrity vs. Mimicry

Fortna finds it "problematic that the rich master, whose oppressive way of life is throughout taken for granted, should in the end become spokesman of the parable's moral."[27] I believe, rather, that it is the listener's work to discern who is spokesperson for the parable. One comes to observe one's own estimate of authority. Is he authoritative who, having identified with exploiting others, exploits? Or does he possess authority who, having access to the sphere of exploitation, refuses? The achievements through mimicry of the first two slaves, although widely applauded, may signify a degree of ongoing enslavement that with irony highlights the autonomy revealed in the last slave's inaction.

To realize that ethical issues are at stake, one has only to contemplate the slave-master's "moral outrage." This man's contempt may be provoked not only by his greed but also by his accurate suspicion that this last slave has indeed read him out for who he is.

Could it be that this parable is evoking, with great sensitivity, the difficult position of a religiously responsive, aristocratic Jew struggling to retain authenticity while immersed in the compromises endemic to the Jewish elites of urban Galilee? Could it be that the last slave's seeming timidity rather represents one person's courageous efforts to retain his ethical footing?

If this is the case, the listener arrives at a place of wonder. How can anyone move in such narrow straits? On the one hand are demands for conformity widespread in a captive upper class overtaken by corruption. On the other hand are this person's still-alive yearnings for integrity. The parable may be capturing his painful dilemma. For the only way out of his slavish mimicry of Rome, the only way back to his Jewish heritage of justice, is to refuse the opportunities of his enslavement. But to reject the exploiter's proffered role of a subordinate exploiter, to disdain the opportunity to imitate, is to provoke anxious ridicule, enraged censure, and eventual ostracism.

Elsewhere Jesus proposes that the destitute are blessed. The reason, according to Crossan,[28] is not because they are better than the rest of us, but because, within the pervasive structures of systemic injustice, they are the only ones left who are innocent.

3

A Slave and a Master

The Gospel context for the Unforgiving Servant asks its hearers to take sides. As the editor of Matthew's Gospel has Jesus say outright,[1] listeners are to emulate the forgiving actions of the slave-master and to condemn the unforgiving slave. Few observers question this well-established distribution of approval and disapproval.

The text used below is one provided by DeBoer (230). In an effort to restore a more original version, he has proposed four changes; these are placed in boldface and explained in the accompanying footnote. In turn, I have replaced DeBoer's use of "servant." The Greek *doulos* means "slave."[2]

The Situation
*A **person** wished to settle accounts with his slaves.*

Scene 1
*a. After he had begun reckoning, one debtor of 10,000 **denarii** was brought to him. And because he was unable to pay up, the master commanded him to be sold, with his wife and children and all that he had, and the sum to be repaid.*
*b. So the slave fell down and was **beseeching** him, saying, "Be patient with me, and I shall repay you everything."*
*c. And the master of that slave was moved to pity and released him and forgave him the **loan**.*

Scene 2

a. That slave went out and found one of his fellow slaves, who owed him 100 denarii, and he grabbed and choked him, saying, "Pay up what you owe."

b. So his fellow slave fell down and was beseeching him, saying, "Be patient with me, and I shall repay you."

c. He did not wish to do so, but went and threw him into prison, until he should pay up what was owed.

Scene 3

a. When his fellow slaves saw what had happened, they were greatly shocked and went and reported to their master all that had happened.

b. Then his master summoned him and said to him, "Evil slave, I forgave you all that debt, since you beseeched me. Was it not necessary also for you to have had mercy on your fellow slave, as I had mercy on you?"

c. And his master became angry and handed him over to the jailers until he should pay up all that was owed. (Matthew 18:23-34)[3]

The next sentence in the text is commentary, which Matthew reports as the words of Jesus: "So also my heavenly Father will do to every one of you [that is, punish you], if you do not forgive your brother from your heart." Many scholars judge this verse to be a Matthean addition.[4]

Yet, as DeBoer observes, this one-sentence commentary has had enormous influence upon all subsequent understandings of this parable:

By means of verse 35 . . . Matthew in effect invites his readers or listeners to interpret the parable allegorically, i.e., to regard the *kyrios* [master] of the parable as God, the "debtor" of v 24 (the *doulos* [slave] of vv 26-28) as a Matthean Christian to whom the merciful God has, through the atoning death of Christ, granted "forgiveness of sins" (26:28), and the *syndoulos* [fellow slaves] of vv 28-30, 33 as Christian *adelphos* [brothers] to whom the Matthean Christian is expected to extend an analogous forgiveness (cf. 5:48). In addition, the fate of the servant in v. 34 is understood as the eternal damnation to be meted out at the final judgment to Christian "servants" . . . who fail to measure up.[5]

Matthew's allegory has remained persuasive for twenty centuries. Although the parable appears to support the allegory's assumptions, namely, an idealizing of the master and a denigration of the slave, there exist, I believe, clues that allow the listener not only to question such assumptions but to create a very different understanding of this story.

The Slave's Motive

One way to enter this narrative is to notice the unforgiving slave's dangerous disregard for his own safety. Although wellplaced and skillful enough to win from his master a huge loan, this highly competent man, concerning a simple matter, makes a disastrous error. In contrast to all of his previous behavior he fails, at this critical moment, to mimic his master. In so doing he predictably enrages a powerful person on whom he is totally dependent. When this slave grabs and chokes his colleague, he has achieved a stunning split in his awareness. Not only is he unable to connect what has just been done for him with what he should now be doing, he also fails to anticipate the obvious retaliation he is provoking. Whether he is given to generosity or not, prudence now dictates he should do everything possible to appear generous.

The listener has the option of moving from being impressed by the slave's failure to imitate his master's generosity (the place where most of the understandings of this story focus) to becoming impressed by the slave's remarkable stupidity.[6] That this competent man's miscalculation is so dangerous suggests both that he has motives other than getting his money back and that these motives are urgent.

> *The master commanded him to be sold, with his wife and children and all that he had. . . . The master was moved to pity and released him and forgave him the loan.*

Listeners tend to savor the brilliant moment of the second sentence and to ignore the vicious realities of the first. But the first represents the totality of the prior experience of both protagonists. Throughout their lives each has served the requirements of a society of slaves and masters. Until now neither has relaxed for a moment the ruthlessness essential to its maintenance. Both, by virtue of their possession of arbitrary power, have long been corrupted in the same way. Each knows well how to shut out fellow feeling in order to crush the weaker delinquent. Such behavior was commonplace up and down the entire social spectrum; no one would have thought to raise a finger in protest.[7]

As a necessary corollary, this slave has always lived with the threat of disaster not only to himself but also to his family, should he fail in his obligations. Knowing no option other than the certainty of power exercised ruthlessly, the slave learned long ago to fit himself to such an expectation; being one who is forever controlled, he will forever control others.

The master of that slave . . . released him and forgave him. . . . That slave went and found one of his fellow slaves . . . and he grabbed and choked him. . . .

A link appears between the last part of the first scene ("released and forgave") and the first part of the second ("grabbed and choked"). It is as if the slave must abruptly grab back what the master has so suddenly released. Here may be a tug-of-war; at stake may be not the repayment of a modest loan but rather the reconstitution of an entire way of life.

When he grabs, chokes, demands, and imprisons, the slave is in fact imitating his master. Yet the person he is mimicking is not his unexpectedly generous "new" master, but rather the one he has always known. The old master, of course, thought nothing of selling a trusted subordinate into a worse slavery,[8] just as the slave now thinks nothing of imprisoning his fellow. The only difference between the two is one of power. Where the slave jails a single colleague, the master was prepared, without concern for the innocence of wife and children, to savage an entire family.

The slave's act of grabbing, moreover, may reveal how he has just experienced his master's release. Having known only ruthless control, he cannot comprehend what has just happened. Where the master believes he has released, the slave may in fact feel swept away—and terrified at being so completely stripped of every certainty. If the world is no longer made up of "users" and "used," of what could it possibly be made?[9] In his confusion, he tries to grab back the only trustworthy way of relating he has ever known.

Schafer offers an observation about psychotherapy that is pertinent here: "It is the unconsciously told narrative that makes intelligible [the client's] having reacted to the event in an extraordinarily angry, agitated and depressed manner."[10] In the present context, the slave's unusually abrupt, mindless, and dangerous action makes sense only if an imagined reality takes precedence over the one immediately apparent.

Here, then, is a first way to comprehend the slave's stupidity. It may be that his behavior has little to do with control over his weaker colleague and far more to do with efforts to restore those long-standing patterns of dominance and submission holding him together with his master. To satisfy his urgent need for continuity, this competent person ignores warnings clamoring for attention, namely, that to survive (through his customary deference) he ought immediately to imitate his new master. The slave's need to have his familiar world back may at this moment be more compelling than considering how to remain safe. Safety as an issue can come into focus only when the means to safety can be imagined.

If the master will not continue in the role of master and maintain for his slave the established order—the order which heretofore has contained all of the possibilities for predictability, then the slave, ignoring his personal safety, will within his constricted imagination attempt to pull that order back into place.

Can the Master Change the World?

The master commanded him to be sold, with his wife and children and all that he had. . . . The master . . . was moved to pity and released him and forgave him the loan. . . . his master became angry and handed him over to the jailers until he should pay up all that was owed.

The rapidity of the master's shifts in mood is astonishing. Scott, when noticing these abrupt reversals, makes his observation at the level of the story's structure.[11] But equally breathtaking is the slave-master's instability at the level of emotional experience. Within a brief span of time this man moves from the cruelty of breaking up a family (brooking no delay), to compassionate forgiveness (providing extraordinary largesse), to vengeful torturing (allowing no escape). How can such disparate attitudes arise in such rapid succession from within the same person?

Both in its novelty and its risk the master has made an extraordinary gesture. His action challenges entrenched practice; among his slave-holding peers he puts his reputation on the line. But the master also appears enticed by the supposed potency of his initiative. His explosive anger at the failure of his generous act suggests how convinced he is of its effectiveness. What may account for his shifting of moods may be a naive expectation born of dominance. For he indeed seems to hope that with a single, masterful stroke he should be able to dent and even flatten those misshapen attitudes hardened into the very foundation of a society of masters and slaves.

Once within his new role of forgiver, the master looks to his action to transform in a moment the heartlessness of a worldview centuries in the making. Within the new, moreover, he retains the old; he remains master. When releasing, he does not wonder or ask; he declares. When forgiving, he stays in control. The slave, as always, remains the one who must adapt.

Weighing Magnanimity against Oppression

Without obvious pressure, this parable demands of the listener an unavoidable decision. How do you weigh an act of unusual magnanimity against centuries of institutional oppression? Or, to put it with more bias, how might the social context of an action eviscerate that action's effectiveness?

One does not have to suppose that the master forgave in order to render his slave a more generous person; nonetheless, both master and many listeners agree that such a transformation ought to occur. Impressed by large differences in money, listeners fail to ponder large differences in power. The irony here may be profound. The master—and many listeners with him—may be saying to the slave, "You should be able to overturn in a moment what I have failed to confront in a lifetime," namely, the unavoidable consequences of one person's ultimate control over the life choices of another.

In his new world of forgiveness, can the master provide his slave with the means to change while still remaining master? The facts of their shared history of dominance and submission together with the master's ongoing control all point to the inability of the master, as master, to produce a new order. The master cannot, in this reading, because the present regime of forgiveness, like the previous regime of dominance, is based on the exercise of power.

Precisely because he acts as master, that is, coercively, the master cannot adopt what may be the only way available to enable another to change, namely, to be aware of and affirm the other's experience. The unilateral nature of the master's initiative ignores his slave's need gradually to come to terms with a strange, dangerous, new way of being. In hoping to evoke a forgiving attitude while still remaining in control, the master may himself have undermined his own potency. Indeed, the master's condemning words, "Was it not necessary for you to have mercy . . . as I had mercy on you?" appear very close to the words the master has just condemned, namely, "Pay up what you owe!"

In the present reading, the slave cannot imitate his master because he cannot conceive—nor can his master provide him any means of conceiving—that he might be other than a slave. Could it be that in the grabbing and choking of his fellow, the slave is trying to say several things at once? First, that he can imagine in this sudden crisis no other way to be than exactly the way he and his master have always been. Second, that something more is required before this matter of forgiveness can succeed, something still owed, not by this other slave, but by the master himself—specifically, that the master reach beyond his exceptional generosity and acknowledge the unchanged consequences of the fact that he still remains master.[12]

At issue here, while certainly not the abolishment of ancient slavery, may be how one takes the measure of its inevitable effects. When the master releases his slave's debt, the listener may be in the presence of a truly remarkable opportunity. For at this moment she or he must decide whether the slave-master's unilateral act of generosity indeed has the power to wrest apart ancient slavery's iron law of ruthlessness.

Guilt Provoking Punishment

The master of that slave . . . released him and forgave him. . . . That slave went out and found one of his fellow slaves . . . and he grabbed and choked him. . . .

There may be another way to comprehend the slave's stupidity. Because he has become unconsciously and intolerably guilty, he sets out to provoke his own punishment. It will take a few paragraphs to make intelligible this second possibility.[13]

Psychoanalysis proposes that one's sense of guilt is the particular anxiety that arises when one hates the person one loves. ("Love" and "hate" are here shorthand terms condensing the wide range of affectionate and aggressive feelings that accompany the two main tasks of human development: relying on another person and becoming separate from that person.)

For example, an early anxiety that takes the form of guilt occurs when a child begins to separate from its mother and move toward its father. At this stage the healthy girl is in conflict between the part of her that wants to deprive her mother of the man she possesses and the part of her that loves her mother and wants her mother's love. Likewise, the healthy boy is in conflict between the part of him that wants to deprive his father of the woman he possesses, and the part of him that loves his father and wants his father's love. Psychoanalytic theory proposes that children, when entering these conflicts, experience a particular anxiety, namely, guilt. The child's ability to hold in awareness representations of both loving and hating the same person—and thus to feel guilty—indicates an important achievement.

I propose that the slave, at the moment of forgiveness, suddenly starts to love the slave-master he has always hated. Such a turn signals an altogether unexpected event. His hate has been so familiar to him as to be unquestioned; he has for so long accepted the safe world provided by the confines of his master's domination that he cannot imagine living outside its definitions. He may hope to overturn his own slavery but not the terms of its underlying ruthlessness. Again, if the world does not consist of those who control and those who are controlled, of what could it possibly consist?

What does the slave do with this utterly new sensation? For he is becoming aware that not only does he want to remain safe in the long-established, coercive world provided by his old master, he also wants to follow his new master, throw off the former definitions, and discover novel ways of relating. In so doing, he enters an arena of unbearable conflict. Toward a person he has always wanted to harm, he abruptly feels affection. As a consequence, he experiences intense guilt.

Winnicott, following Freud, further suggests that actual crime is often not the cause of guilt-feeling; rather it is the result of guilt.[14] That is, a crime (the slave's cashiering of his fellow slave) may represent an effort to find some reason for an earlier, inarticulate but pressing sense of guilt. Here that earlier guilt would be the overwhelming anxiety the slave feels when abruptly stimulated to love the master he had always hated.

Because he feels so unbearably guilty, and because he lacks any way to express this ambivalence in words, the slave without thinking provokes retaliation. He is reduced to engineering a false punishment for daring to agree that he wants release, not simply from the debt but also from the hatred he has always known.

So he grabs and chokes his fellow in full view. At great cost to himself and pain to his lord, he brings his disappointed master crashing down upon him. Unable to tolerate his appreciation for being so released, he inspires the other's anger in order to crush the guilty longing he has momentarily allowed to take on life within himself.[15]

The moment the listener supposes that the slave's stupid response has no easy explanation, she or he is positioned to raise new questions. Yet many are tempted, following both the master and the editor of Matthew, to fill this gap by perceiving the unforgiving slave as merely wanton.

But such listeners are caught in a trap. They are supporting (alongside the master) the very act the master is condemning, namely, the unforgiving imprisoning of another for a failed obligation. Only this time the debt owed is not 100 denarii but rather that the slave imitate, whether he is ready to or not, the master's unexpected generosity. Together with the slave-master, these listeners say to the unforgiving slave, "I will ignore your capacities and desires in favor of my own. I will imprison you until you repay an obligation I have without warning or preparation decided to enforce. I will do to you exactly what I am punishing you for having done."

Anger Contrasted with Grief

The parable portrays another way of responding to the unfortunate slave's unforgiving behavior. This alternate portrayal leads to a second major gap in this narrative—one that is difficult to notice.

> *When his fellow slaves saw what had happened, they were greatly shocked. . . . And his master became angry. . . .*

The surprising nature of the fellow slaves' response is blunted by DeBoer's rendering, which has it that they were "greatly shocked." A more detailed translation better reveals this second gap, namely, the striking contrast between the master's response of anger (in the Greek, *orgistheis:* being angry, indignant, wrathful) and the fellow slaves' parallel but very different response of becoming extremely grieved (*elupaithaisan:* they were grieved, sad, sorrowful, distressed; *sphodra:* very [much], extremely, greatly). This difference, of potential significance, is seldom noted and rarely probed.

As suggested above, the coercion hidden in the master's forgiveness is revealed in his subsequent anger. This anger prevents him from becoming curious about his slave's stupidity. A grieving response, by contrast, might not. Grieving might even have allowed the master some access to his own vulnerability, namely, his capacity to be hurt by his slave's rejection.

Smaller gaps exist within the construct "grieving." For which slave—or both—are the fellow slaves so distressed? Certainly they may be sad for their imprisoned companion. They may well be distressed by anticipating the loss of further magnanimity in their lord. But what are their feelings for the oppressor slave himself?

It is hard to stay with this question; it is easier to assume that the fellow slaves share their master's anger. Listeners are tempted to elevate the fellow slaves to the master's social level and imagine that they too wish to enforce retribution. Put another way, listeners are tempted to identify with the power of the master rather than recall the pervasive emasculation of the slave group. Most of these slaves were seldom able to intervene with their masters through self-initiated, self-directed action; they were instead limited to compliance and observation. We may find it difficult to imagine the feelings of persons so regularly compelled to passivity.[16]

Nonetheless, the parable offers this seemingly small, obscure moment to engage in large wonder. Unlike their master in power, the fellow slaves are not outraged; rather they are caught up in grief.

In a society of slaves and masters, the slave is obliged to understand and comply with the master's experience; the master is under no such reciprocal obligation. In such an environment there are only good and bad slaves, never good and bad masters—if "good" and "bad" are limited to describing one's obligations to know and accept another person's experience. Such is the tyranny of these social conventions that modern listeners, freed from their actual constraints, still do not readily question their effects. Few suspect that the master has somehow contributed to the tragedy at hand. Few suppose that the unforgiving slave may be less than fully responsible for his fate.

Could it be, as the fellow slaves consider the position of their abusive colleague, that they are aware of a shared propensity toward what might be termed a "kick-the-dog" syndrome? That is, since I dare not abuse my apparently forgiving but in some way still abusive master, I will instead express my emotions toward a more innocent and less powerful colleague. Could it further be that these same slaves have some empathy for the sequence of events now lodged by the slave-master in their fellow, namely, of a lifetime of control followed by the disorienting terror of sudden release?

Perhaps they perceive, having themselves lived their lives in positions of powerlessness, how their colleague has been abruptly torn by massive contradictions. How the one imposing them has felt no obligation to be aware of their effect. How their fellow has just had to endure the threat of even further enslavement and then the sudden withdrawal of that threat—not unlike the last-minute reprieve from execution by firing squad that Fyodor Dostoevsky had to spend the rest of his life trying to comprehend. How, as a result, he may temporarily have lost all sense of direction. Perhaps they can feel, if not describe, the inner workings of this tragedy: that for a moment their colleague was simply out of control, overwhelmed with the powerful urge to throttle someone—someone he can no longer identify.

But then, some may respond, if the fellow slaves understood all these things, why, grieving as they were, did they turn their colleague in? Here is another shift difficult to comprehend: from grieving to reporting. The listener may ponder this perplexing gap. How does this change occur? How do the fellow slaves move from private distress to public accusation?

The answer most ready to hand, of course, is that they identify with their roughed-up colleague who has just been jailed. They want the master to correct that injustice. Like siblings who enact upon each other the conflicts of their parents, they offer up their displaced struggle with their fellow to a compromised judge whom they still hope will set things right. But might the more discerning among them, in their grief, also suppose some larger dimensions troubling their master's newfound, fragile initiative? Could these slaves, wholly dependent on their master's moods, fear for his vulnerability? That is, could they estimate that hidden within the master's forgiveness is not only the potential for a new way of being but also a readiness to collapse? That their colleague's provocative act might so sully the master's initiative as to cause him to regress—or worse, to harden? Do they then report to their master as a means to discover the outcome of their awful suspicion?

Or do they, joining their disgraced colleague, want to restore the ruthlessness that has always heretofore undergirded the security of their world? Or perhaps they simply anticipate, as do many listeners, the outrage of the master—which in turn relieves the story of its tension. Or could they, in their grieving, be wanting with hopeful uncertainty to test the further resources of their master's unanticipated forgiveness, so that they imagine their lord capable of more penetrating action? Perhaps they then hope for a generous discipline that would reveal a larger understanding of both the culprit's dilemma and the master's own.

Given the greater ambiguities residing in grief (as opposed to anger), the listener here wanders among a multitude of choices.

The Listener's Decision

There may be a crucial difference between the responses of the master and those of the fellow slaves. The master, early on, is "moved to pity." The fellow slaves, in their turn, are "extremely grieved." In being moved to pity, the master may hope to move the slave into some new state. In feeling grieved, the fellow slaves make uncertain moves toward both master and colleague. Their response, lacking in direction, is less confident and more present. Which attitude—coercive compassion or confused grief—is in the end more conducive to uncovering a capacity to forgive?

The parable invites the listener to make some decision about what constitutes forgiveness and how it may be fairly won. The listener is called upon to wonder whether to derive hope from the slave-master's magnificent generosity. One may discern that this remarkable initiative, when left unexamined in its present social context, generates a distorted ambition, which in turn engenders a terrifying uncertainty and from there provokes a disappointed rage. Caught in such a vortex, one comes full circle, back to condemning the forgiven person—and back to doing precisely what one has just condemned. Or the listener may decide to join the fellow-slaves and become simultaneously grief-stricken and accusing.

Held among such alternatives, the listener may experience difficulty in being angry and sad at the same time. Such a listener may then decide to grieve for one slave, for both, or together for slaves and master. Unable to intervene to make things right, this listener, by standing with the fellow slaves somewhere between master and colleague, may find ways both to feel more deeply and to ponder more steadily the perplexities of an adequate forgiveness.

Forgiving and Psychotherapy

To provide added dimensions to the dilemmas facing master, slave, and listener, I want here to offer, in schematic outline, an understanding from within psychotherapy of the process of forgiving.[17] Such work may partly be defined as a person's coming to accept his own capacity to do to others what was once done to him.

Psychotherapists believe it difficult for someone to forgive another without the participation of a third person. Lacking the presence of this third, the one who has been hurt has few resources to reexperience the original pain in such a way that it can be endured, and to explore that reawakened trauma in observing rather than self-protecting and consequently obscuring ways.

This third person must be someone who is not the true source of the hurt but still allows the injured person to relive that hurt. This vital role of representing the originally hurtful person—without in reality being hurtful—is sometimes filled by a psychotherapist.

A client who has experienced abuse in his past gradually discovers, as he develops a sense of safety, a desire to abuse his therapist. Because he has begun to trust his therapist, a client may feel secure enough to try to hurt her. Such an intention, properly understood, has the potential to become an ongoing step in an effort at forgiveness.

For a long time the client is unable to control this impulse to hurt. The therapist, with combined tolerance and toughness allows the attacks (expressed at a verbal level only). Crucial to permitting the client to feel hurtful is the therapist's refusal to retaliate. Without either gratifying or condemning these spoken actions, the therapist tries to survive them.

In turn the client enables the therapist feelingly to understand what the client has earlier experienced. The therapist encounters the same forces that once assaulted and confused the client. She feels sheltered, loved, seduced, made anxious, betrayed, deceived, and devastated by replicas of those same distorted behaviors so destructive in the client's past. Instead of responding to these chaotic behaviors as if they were intended personally, the therapist tries first to survive and then to describe what the client will gradually come to recognize as reenactments—needed because still lacking are words sufficient to comprehend what until now has remained too troubling to be described.

During this extended period, the client slowly puts together two parts of a conflict which up until now he has had to keep apart: (1) that he indeed intends, by his own choice, to hurt his therapist, and (2) that at the same time he has regard for, or loves, the therapist he is attacking.

In this new interpersonal environment, where the therapist allows, and the client achieves, the experience of simultaneously loving and hating the same person, a novel event may occur. This event has the potential both for greater acceptance of oneself in the present and for revising one's experience of the past. The client becomes aware that what the hated (and loved) person of the past did to him he is now doing to the therapist. Put differently, by allowing the client to reenact some version of the original hurt, the therapist is opening a way for the client to realize that he also has the capacity to act as did that person who originally hurt him.

Becoming able to acknowledge his desire to hurt someone he loves, and aware that he cannot easily control these wishes, the client discovers, in feeling terms, that those vicious and uncontrolled behaviors he has always felt as coming at him from the outside are also alive within himself. In consternation the client reports, "What she did to me, and I have always detested, I now see I am doing to you!" The client discovers he has become a version of that person he has up to now hated and blamed.

By realizing his own temptation in the present to hurt others the way someone in the past hurt him, the client attains resources for greater acceptance of, or forgiveness of, both his own harmful intentions and those of his abuser.

The client in time may also realize an emotionally powerful corollary, namely, that this hated person, who caused so much damage to him, was herself enmeshed in this same process of having been hurt and then wanting to hurt another. "I now know that I lose control in ways similar to hers. Now I can feel a little of what it must have been like to be her."

Essential to this growing awareness has been the therapist's earlier allowing of the client's attacks. This permission is not a condoning. Instead, the therapist has been engaged in a nonblaming effort to permit expression of the client's necessary emotions. Forms of the hurting have had to be allowed and then held in awareness until both the one doing the hurting (the client—and sometimes the therapist) and the one being hurt (the therapist—and sometimes the client) can feel it, tolerate it, understand it, and describe it in words.

In sum, because the client has experienced empathy from the therapist, he is better able to extend empathy both to himself and, possibly, to the abusing—and earlier abused—other.

Two completing steps remain: the one who did the hurting (the client—and sometimes the therapist) must now make a repairing gesture that acknowledges having caused the hurt, and the one hurt (the therapist—and sometimes the client) must accept that gesture. This repairing effort and its reciprocal acceptance completes an interaction that earlier, because of the abused person's helplessness and the abuser's denial, could not take place.

This process proceeds along a broken and uncertain course. Its various steps have to be repeated many times. But forgiveness, or acceptance, may be on the way to being accomplished.[18]

The above process of forgiving may be understood as the reversal of a process that takes hold whenever one person controls another.

If someone is too intensely controlled, she cannot achieve a sense of guilt leading to the capacity to make repairs. (Guilt is here understood once again as that particular anxiety a person experiences when she is able at the same time both to have concern for and to want to hurt a significant other person.) Instead of holding on to such an awareness—that the loved person and the controlling person are one and the same—the one controlled learns to love at one time and hate at another. That is, she divides her experience into two separate, unintegrated parts: an idealized world, divorced from reality, which becomes all good, and another world, also divorced from reality, into which everything bad is projected. Her experience then remains split between idealized others and bad others. Once she has with certainty identified those outsiders as bad, the way is open for her to avoid feeling guilty. Rather than struggling with the task of loving and hating at the same time, this person simply scapegoats the outsider. "They" become bad and "we" become good. As a corollary, this same person believes it inconceivable that she could become as hurtful as those outsiders have been to her.[19]

Forgiving While Controlling

We may now use these summaries of the later, reversing process of forgiving, and the earlier process of segregating experience into "bad" and "good" to take further measure of the slave-master's efforts to forgive.

Following a lifetime of being controlled, the slave has split his world into all-good and all-bad. Unable at the same time to hate and love the one above him, he has regularly scapegoated those below him.

The master's abrupt forgiveness shatters the slave's longstanding, predictable, and therefore safe environment. Decades of dominance have rendered the slave unable to hold on to the fact that the forgiving master and the controlling master are one and the same person. Instead, by his action of grabbing and choking, the slave maintains his split-apart experience. He thereby restores the ruthless exercise of power that has always contained all the elements of reliable prediction. By attacking his peer, he restores his split-apart world.[20]

Listeners often assume that the slave should be able at once to bring together these split-apart segments of his world, and that the master has already done all that is necessary to facilitate such a reuniting. I believe otherwise. I think that the parable, with pervasive irony, is exploring the difficulties of effecting forgiveness when one person still controls another.

Permeated by the parasitic values of imperial Rome, the master's environment provides him with few resources to become feelingly aware of the effects of his control over his fellow. Societal norms, in the guise of Roman law, have succeeded in muting protest from either exploiter or victim. In his abrupt and gracious act, the master has crossed into a no-man's land. Little in the law that supports his long-standing dominance is capable of rendering effective his newly discovered generosity.

Since the master's forgiveness lacks a prior feeling of guilt, he is unable to bring together the effects of his sudden compassion with the effects of his chronic dominance. He simply assigns such backbreaking work to his subordinate. The master releases his slave's debt without acknowledging his own, namely, his obligation to recognize the consequences for forgiveness of his longstanding choice to control.

By remaining the sole arbiter of the new order as well as the old, the master excludes any experience other than his own. By dictating rather than participating, he permits only compliance. By his graciousness, he distances himself further from the realities of his own dominance. By exposing nothing in himself for which he, the master, must make restitution, he gives his slave no room to become directly enraged. In the briefest terms, the master cannot succeed in his effort at forgiveness until he finds some way to welcome his slave's hatred.

The master's manner of acting, surely appropriate to the behavior of slave-masters, is ill-fitted to the work of forgiving. The master's attitude collapses at least two potentials vital to any forgiveness: (1) by concealing an ongoing control within his generosity, the master renders even more improbable any possibility that he, the master, might allow—and thereby transform—the slave's hatred of his continuing dominance; and (2) the master's inability to acknowledge his (now disguised and hidden) control reduces further any chance the slave himself might have to make repairs. The master behaves as if there is no lapse on his side for which the slave, in his turn, might offer forgiveness.[21] The master's generosity, when separated from acknowledgment of his ongoing dominance, renders the recipient resourceless. The process is totally, inexorably one-way.

Approached in these terms, the problems the parable offers are formidable. How indeed does one bring together the open-ended process of forgiveness with the controlling behaviors of masters and slaves? How is it possible to move the master's magnificent effort across the large gulf between the world of slavery, with its single alternative of compliance, and the world of forgiveness, where coercion necessarily dissolves in favor of first experiencing and then acknowledging how the other person feels? Is there in fact any way to introduce coercively an attitude of non-coercion? How far, then, might the master's final, impotent rage be from its true source? How can the master possibly recognize the effects of his immersion in the unquestioned corruption of a society based on slavery?

Forgiving and Equality

Because each parable character can see only his own side, this narrative as it stands meets with failure. If the therapist stays only on one side of the client's conflict, the therapy is also likely to stall or collapse. Similarly, if the listener simply idealizes the superior character, then the tension of the parable is released and the parable, for that listener, ends. Both processes—interpretive splitting and psychological splitting—foreclose opportunities to accept alien aspects either of oneself or of another. Both processes may prevent forgiveness.

The slave has to hate not simply the fact of being dominated but also his master's inability to acknowledge guilt about being the one in control. Having no room to express his hatred, the slave has no way to imagine his own capacity to dominate his master. Lacking the means to realize such a potential to do to his lord exactly what his lord has for so long done to him, he has no route open toward discovering his own guilt and thus toward forgiving his master—and hence no way in turn to accept his master's forgiveness. What the master prevents the slave from experiencing, namely, his own wish to dominate the one who has dominated him, is precisely what the slave without understanding enacts upon his weaker fellow. The one hurting and the one hurt never become equal—and thereby reciprocal; instead, the anger is passed on to those below. The whole affair becomes an unyielding, downward spiral.[22]

One can forgive, I believe, only out of an awareness of being in the position of the other who hurts. Put another way, forgiveness must be built upon a prior emotional equality; otherwise "forgiveness" becomes a maddening and hateful cover-up. But how is either participant in the parable, lacking a present, observant third person—such as a listener—to develop this awareness?

4

A Widow and a Judge and Tenant Farmers and a Landlord: A Beginning Inquiry

Each of the parables in this book presents complex interactions compressed within condensed narratives. Two of them, however, carry this combination of complexity within condensation to an extreme. In the first, usually named the Unjust Judge and here titled a Widow and a Judge, an almost resourceless woman confronts a powerful, nearly implacable man. In the second, usually titled the Wicked Tenants and here called Tenant Farmers and a Landlord, a trusting vineyard owner fails to anticipate the murderous intent of distant tenant farmers. These two parables, placed side by side, read as follows:

The Situation

(b)In a certain city there was a judge who neither feared God nor had respect for people	*(a) There was a [good]*[1] *man who owned a vineyard.*
(a) In the same city there was a widow	*(b) He leased it to tenant farmers so they might work it and he might collect the produce from them.*

Scene 1

who kept coming to him and saying, "Grant me justice against my opponent."	*He sent his slaves so that the tenants might give him the produce of the vineyard.*

Scene 2

For a while he refused;	*They seized his slave and beat him, all but killing him. The slave went back and told his master. The master said, "Perhaps [they] did not recognize [him]."[2] He sent another slave. The tenants beat this one as well.*

Scene 3

but later he said to himself, "Though I have no fear of God and no respect for anyone, yet because this widow keeps bothering me, I will grant her justice, so that she may not wear me out by continually coming." (Luke 18:2b-5)[3]	*Then the owner sent his son and said, "Perhaps they will show respect to my son." Because the tenants knew it was he who was the heir to the vineyard, they seized him and killed him. (Gospel of Thomas 65)[4]*

I have juxtaposed these narratives because they have a similar content—although very different outcomes. They place respect for the dignity of human beings in tension with the use of raw power. Taken together, I believe they are exploring the limits of law. In one a supposedly law-abiding judge enjoys a perverse but disciplined disrespect for law. In the other, an absentee landlord, respecting law, reaps tragedy. By looking at both parables at once, the reader can compare a lack of respect for law arising from a remarkable self-centeredness with an expectation of respect for law arising from a remarkable self-centeredness.

Unlike our other five parables, these two provide no spoken dialogue; give and take is replaced by monologue or wordless action. Their economy of line matches the etchings of Picasso or the cutouts of Matisse. An enormous amount is left unarticulated; as a consequence, the gaps that the listener must fill with meaning are greatly expanded.

This apparent paucity of meaning led very early to the importation of meaning from the outside. Starting at least with the Gospel editors, a Widow and a Judge was taken, without a trace of irony, to point to the opposite of what it describes, while Tenant Farmers and a Landlord was submerged in the assumption that Jesus had created an allegory about his own execution.

Much of what happens in these two stories is not described, and much of what is described makes little sense. When extracted from the contexts supplied by the Gospel editors, these stories appear either meaningless or bizarre. One major commentator concludes a long and thoughtful chapter on Tenant Farmers and a Landlord with these words: "The parable frustrates not only allegory but also any effort to make sense of it!"[5]

Of the parables in this book I found these two the most daunting. I have been much aided by exploring analogues between the situations in these narratives and the situation in psychotherapy. My comments are organized under six headings divided into two chapters.

In this chapter I explore how differences between the parable characters result in the creation of separate imaginative worlds. In the next chapter, using therapist techniques of listening, I invite the parable listener to enter and inhabit these very different worlds.

Barriers to Understanding

The characters in the parables are separated by differences in social and economic power; the participants in psychotherapy are separated by differences in anxiety. As a consequence, each misperceives the other.

Even when these narratives end, the underlying differences that support their conflicts continue. One side (the judge or the landlord) still possesses almost all of the power. The other side (the widow or the tenants), although temporarily successful, reverts to powerlessness. Solid barriers to mutual understanding remain.

These barriers involve immense differences in social position, political influence, economic security, and the ability to use physical force. The judge is literate, has political connections, and is close to the center of power. The widow is probably illiterate and clearly lacks political influence. The distant landlord does not work his land yet claims a large share of its produce and all of its security; the tenants have no hope of possessing the land and, in consequence, no confident enjoyment of the results of their labor. [6] In both parables the opposing protagonists live in hugely different worlds, worlds that barely touch, and then touch only at one narrow point.

Turning to psychotherapy, it is the presence of anxiety that separates the two participants. With anxiety revealed in their symptoms, clients come to therapists. Once in therapy, older areas of anxiety are broached. Given the earlier contexts of danger that gave birth to their symptoms, it is no surprise that clients respond with renewed anxiety to the recreation of these older contexts. Only gradually does the client entrust such exquisitely vulnerable areas to the developing space of wonder; much of the time misperception is rife.

Speechlessness Enhancing Distortion

Because of the large differences between them, neither person can speak clearly to the other. This inability sustains their misperceptions.

Across the social distance separating them, neither protagonist in either parable has any ready way to speak to the other. Communication is instead squeezed through the narrow confines of inarticulate action. Thoughtful speech is replaced by curt demands; wounds overwhelm words. Misunderstandings lead to escalations couched in ambiguous behaviors—resulting in further misunderstandings.

The widow in a Widow and a Judge, frustrated by the judge's refusal to recognize her, is compelled to become a battering ram. The Greek verb *hupopiadzo,* translated here as "wearing out" (the judge says, "I will grant her justice, so that she may not wear me out by continually coming"), literally means "to strike under the eye." The image comes from boxing. The verb places the widow in a boxing ring, jabbing repeatedly at the eye socket of the judge.

Perhaps she began with reasoned arguments. But not any more. Because no patient, resonating listener has responded, she is reduced to fewer words and more constricted words. These words, in turn, are robbed of their potency by the blocked ears of the judge. His resistance renders her progressively more incompetent. In the end, her severely limited action, like David's small stone in the narrowly exposed forehead of the armored Goliath, succeeds in breaking through only miraculously.

Reasons for the speechlessness in Tenant Farmers and a Landlord are more difficult to grasp. The tenants express their disdain for all to see on the bloodied bodies of the landlord's slaves. Yet such acts of violence provoke in the landlord no demand for explanation. Where the widow lacks social standing, the landlord has society's law as his platform. How is it he fails to force his insulting subordinates to declare themselves in words?

Whatever the landlord's reasons (and there may be some, to be explored later), both parables insist that the opening for spoken communication is exceedingly narrow. Discourse, listening, give and take—in short, all the normal means of exposing and resolving differences—are excised. Distortions multiply unimpeded by description.

The following paragraphs outline some of the ways in which the characters in these two parables might go about frustrating the establishment of clear, consensual meaning. The judge or the landlord might deceive himself as follows:

> As the more powerful person, not only can I refuse to empathize with the experience of those who must depend on me, I can also force them to comply with my own perception of who I am. I can then further my misunderstanding by proceeding to believe in the compliance I have coerced. Thus, for example, I, the judge, can deceive myself into thinking that the woman whom I force to keep coming before me is interested in who I am. Thus, for example, I, the landlord, can deceive myself into believing that my tenant farmers want to abide by the contract I have imposed.

This double deception—coercing compliance and then believing in it—is how I prevent myself from empathizing with my subordinate's experience. Sealed off from such observation, I do not come in contact with different perspectives; I am free to maintain my imaginative world as I please.

The above paragraphs can be rewritten to accommodate the subordinate. The widow or the tenant farmers might speak as follows:

> As the subordinate person, I can avoid clear communication with my superior by appearing to agree with the definitions he imposes. But I can go further. I can increase our mutual misunderstanding by accepting these distorting definitions of who I am. Thus, for example, I, the deprived widow, can come to believe I deserve the abuse I am experiencing. Thus, for example, we, the

rebellious tenants, can become so convinced we are unrecogniz-
able that we can imagine murder as the only means available to
gain recognition. We have reached the point of rejecting any information that disrupts these convictions.

Because of these insistent distortions, neither parable character has
access to the very different imaginative world of the other.

In psychotherapy, because premature clarity would too abruptly
reawaken ancient terrors, the therapist must not yet name, and the client
cannot yet tolerate, any more accurate description of what may be occur-
ring between them. Both therapist and client respect the anxiety aroused
when engaged in a cautious probing of those areas of danger where the
distortions originally formed.[7]

Nonetheless, each person—parable character with parable character,
client with therapist—somehow must create some kind of meaning.
Each, then, is tempted to create meanings that rely on imaginative con-
structions having little to do with the experience of the other.

The Absence of Outside Authority

*The setting allows no outside authority to come in and put things right;
the two persons must cope as best they can by themselves.*

When these two parables are compared, their endings seem arbitrary.
Little in the similar processes of either appears to predict their very different outcomes.

The judge has no respect for the widow's rights under law. The tenants
have no respect for the landlord's rights under law. Confronting lawlessness in the judge, the widow resorts to further initiative—and wins. Confronting lawlessness among his tenants, the landlord resorts to further
initiative—and loses.

Both widow and landlord are taking huge risks. But why the different
outcomes? Why should the lawless judge vindicate the persistent
widow's cause while the lawless tenants murder the persistent landlord's
son? Why does the self-centered judge, instead of engaging in further
bullying, capitulate? Why do the rebellious tenants, instead of continuing to wound, risk murder? What discernible fact in either parable pre-
dicts that the widow will win and the landlord will lose?

This undermining of predictable sequence is, for both parables, based on the exclusion of law; access to external authority is cut off. In the first, the judge's obstinate indifference, unchallenged, progressively constricts the widow's badgering; in the second, the landlord's stubborn obtuseness, uncorrected, exacerbates the tenants' hostility. Throughout this steady increase in misunderstanding, no third person is allowed in to describe their differences. The two parties must cope by themselves as best they can.

At the outset of a Widow and a Judge, listeners are introduced to a sitting judge. By definition a judge cannot decide disputes by himself but rather must interpret the community's intention. In the Jewish culture of this story, this intention is defined as the will of God; someone filling the role of judge is required to "fear God."

Yet this judge does not fear God. He cannot exercise judgeship because he has access to no perspective other than his own; he stands obligated to no tradition. Further, he possesses no capacity for empathy; he has "no respect for anyone." Thus, he is devoid, first from without and then from within, of any reference points other than his own desire. Behind a facade of commitment to law, this judge is subject to neither external rule nor internal conscience. The story, in turn, firmly prevents anyone from challenging this corruption.[8]

Within Tenant Farmers and a Landlord, the absence of law is uncovered more gradually. Indeed, the landlord becomes aware of it only after the story ends; his realization will occur later, in a flash of brutal, devastating illumination. During those brief moments all the certain conventions in the secure world of that good man will be forever shattered.

But at the beginning of the narrative, everything seems well in hand. If there is any disaffection among his tenants, the landlord is unaware of it. In spite of mounting evidence to the contrary, he remains convinced that they want to honor their contract. In his eyes his own profits are not too high, he is not an exploiter, and the tenants have not been coerced by economic hardship into compliance. The landlord persists in believing that there is no reason for rebellion.

Calmly, the landlord seems subject to forces wildly out of control. Twice the tenants broadcast their hostility; twice the landlord insists that the bloody wounds of his slaves are evidence of misunderstanding. He appears determined not to see what they are shoving in his face. Throughout the growth of this lethal denial, no outsider is allowed in to warn him of the enormity of his error.

This lack in either story of someone able to name what is happening is unusually compelling. The tension aroused in the listener by these two distressed parties trapped together without relief may be part of the reason why each story has attracted such definitive emendation from the outside. I believe that those components designed to reduce this tension are in fact supplied by later editors. Jesus rarely if ever appears himself to have resolved the difficulties his parables create. Where such resolution occurs, also apparent are the marks of a later hand.[9]

For both these stories, the Gospel writers propose that Jesus provides what seem to be resolutions, which, on examination, neither response comes close to supplying: For a Widow and a Judge, Jesus' supposed final commentary draws one away from the criminal judge and toward the beneficent figure of God. Even if there is no direct transformation, the listener, distracted, no longer experiences the unendurable environment of lawlessness:

And the Lord said, "Listen to what the unjust judge says. And will not God grant justice to his chosen ones who cry to him day and night? Will he delay long in helping them? I tell you, he will quickly grant justice to them." (Luke 18:6-8a)

As an underwater swimmer breaks to the surface straining for air, so the editor reaches to grasp some other presence to overcome the suffocating exclusion locked into this parable. The lawless, self-centered bully of a judge is suddenly replaced; in his stead is revealed a deeply concerned deity. Thus, the Lukan context, by violating a carefully fabricated limit, attempts to pull the parable inside out. Nowhere in the narrative itself, however, is there any hint of such a resolution. Nothing in the story suggests access to another world, a different regime, a new law. Yet the urgency created by its limit is so compelling that one longs to import an outside authority.

For Tenant Farmers and a Landlord, Jesus supposedly states that the landlord murders the tenants (an outcome not provided in Thomas):

"What then will the owner of the vineyard do? He will come and destroy the tenants and give the vineyard to others." (Mark 12:9)

"What then will the owner of the vineyard do to them? He will come and destroy those tenants and give the vineyard to others." (Luke 20:15b-16a)

Matthew places this vengeful climax not on Jesus' lips but in the imagination of the parable's early listeners:

"Now when the owner of the vineyard comes, what will he do to those tenants?" They said to him, "He will put those wretches to a miserable death, and lease the vineyard to other tenants who give him the produce at the harvest time." (Matthew 21:40-41)

This kind of ending, however, makes no change in the misperceptions lodged between landlord and tenants; it merely eradicates them. That such an undemanding, uncreative resolution could have been an original part of this complex parable is difficult to imagine.[10]

Within the limits of both stories, is there is in fact any way for its participants to escape their mutual misperceptions? The only movement possible, in the absence of law, may be repetition. The widow's pounding, in a context devoid of respect, is her only alternative. Although such persistence might seem to effect change, in fact it does not; persistence evokes merely a reciprocal stubbornness or, in the end, a compliance devoid of change. Similarly, the tenants repeatedly wound, and the landlord repeatedly tolerates the wounding. The son's murder can be understood as an extension of this repetition; it is more of the same, enlarged.

The possibility for a true ending, for a resolution through some kind of dialogue leading to mutual understanding and thus to transformation, is absent. The judge recognizes neither his failure to own the obligations of his chosen role nor his disguised desire for human contact. The widow remains deprived of rightful resources. Neither landlord nor tenants change. The former continues to insist on the lawfulness of unjust laws, while the latter remain reduced to violence.

These two parables insist on enclosing their listeners in painfully repetitive environments. Whoever enters their space is overtaken by an urgent desire to break apart their boundaries in order to introduce some outside authority.

The environment of psychotherapy is similarly limited, similarly pressured by repeated longings that the therapist relieve the pain, and similarly devoid of an external savior. Such limitation is not readily apparent—most often not to the client and sometimes not to the therapist.

The client, filled with anxiety, understandably resists engaging in the slow and difficult work of discovering and naming what the trouble is. This resistance comes because the main function of that anxiety has been all along to warn the client to stay away from what was earlier, whether in imagination or in fact, truly terrifying. The therapist understands that the client's anxiety will fuel a myriad of strategies designed to avoid collaboration and instead to cajole answers from the outside. Nonetheless, therapists are at times hard pressed not to be overtaken by such longings. Pressed by both the client's distress and the client's hope, the therapist is sometimes tempted to behave as if actually in possession of answers.[11]

Yet, where the world of the client is concerned, the therapist is called upon to know that she does not know. Whatever discoveries are made, whatever resolutions are achieved, will be accomplished through hardwon collaboration. There is no one out there who can simply walk in and set things right.

The Creation of Alien Worlds

The inability to speak accurately results in the development of symptoms, that is, of inarticulate enactments that disguise meaning and appear as puzzling behaviors. These symptoms reveal how, in isolation, each partner has created an internal, imaginative world that is very different from the imaginative world of the person with whom they are trying to interact. It is within these private, imaginative worlds that the behaviors of their occupants, so perplexing to outsiders, make sense.

When important emotions are experienced as too dangerous to be described, they are often enacted. The child who cannot say why he is angry or, even more, that he is angry, sometimes sets fires. In these parables the pressing inability to speak reduces complex expression into impoverished actions—snarling, silence, wounding, and murder—actions that in turn undermine the remaining possibilities for speech. As a consequence, it becomes very difficult to grasp what may really be going on.

It is not at all clear why the judge, so committed to individualism as to reject his tradition, should devote his life to a public office designed to foster that tradition. One views the risk-taking persistence of the widow with amazement. It is very hard to understand how the landlord can send his son unprotected into almost certain danger. One has great difficulty imagining how the tenants can believe their murderous behavior will lead to a secure future.

Parable listeners, like therapists and archaeologists, have available only shards; they are left with the work of reconstructing the whole from the disconnected fragments available. As an archaeologist attempts to reconstruct an entire vessel from such shards, so the listener may attempt to infer from the seemingly incomprehensible behaviors of the parable participants the larger inner, imaginative worlds in which those actions make sense.

What makes a symptom unintelligible to participant and observer alike is the absence of a historical context in which to place it. One has yet to discover how and when, as these persons tried to relate, their puzzling ways of behaving had their origins.

We may begin by noting that central to both parables is a tension within their various imaginative worlds between "recognizing" and "having respect for." For example, the judge recognizes that his community's law is based on its fear of God but has no respect for any of it; the tenants recognize the identity of the landowner's son but obviously do not respect him.

The verb in scene 3 of Tenant Farmers and a Landlord, "show respect for," is a translation of the Coptic of the Gospel of Thomas, which in turn is a translation of the lost original Greek. In the other three extant versions of this story, the relevant verb form in Greek is identical: *entrapaisontai*. The landlord says of his tenants, ". . . they will show respect for my son. . . ." In a Widow and a Judge, the parallel verb in scene 3 is *entrepomai*. The judge says, "I have . . . no respect for anyone. . . ." Both verb forms are derived from *entrepo*, which means either (1) to make (someone) ashamed, or be put to shame, or (2) to have regard for, respect. The double meanings in English capture well the relationship between showing respect for someone and the ability to feel shame.

Neither judge nor tenants feel shame; each has lost that capacity essential to its experience, namely, respect for others.

But here the listener comes upon a growing, surprising awareness: could it be that the widow and the landlord are also unable to respect the different perspectives of the judge and the tenants?

Neither the widow nor the landlord follows the judge and the tenants in refusing to abide by law. But ambiguity resides in how both show respect for the refusal of their opponents to subject themselves to law. The widow's persistent belief in the judge's respect for law reveals either marked naiveté or else considerable courage in so exposing herself to retribution. The landlord's insistence that his tenants are respecting their contractual obligations reveals his denial of the obvious alternative, namely, that others less fortunate than he might perceive a difference between what is lawful and what is just. It does not occur to this good man that he might be perpetrating, in the eyes of his tenants, an injustice. As a consequence he fails to evaluate accurately the dangerous forces assembling against him.

Given the absence of respect for law in their opponents, neither widow nor landlord can be at all certain of the outcome of their persistent reliance on law. The widow could have as easily been harmed as vindicated by the judge—who certainly possessed resources to hurt equal to those of the tenants.

Where do the widow and the landlord discover the means to take such large risks?

The ability to recognize difference but not respect the fact of its separate reality has the capacity to foster amazing sequences inside our imagination. We turn now to explore in these two parables how such self-deceptions might be nurtured and sustained.

5

A Widow and a Judge and Tenant Farmers and a Landlord: Further Inquiry

Using "Transference" to Understand Alien Worlds

The parable listener is invited to enter into the separate and different imaginative worlds of widow, judge, tenants, and landlord. This section offers the first of two ways of listening given to psychotherapists that may be of use in this task: therapists assume that all of us, regularly and inappropriately, expect important people in our present to behave toward us as did important people in our past.

A further analogue to parable listening may be derived from the single most important way a psychotherapist listens: the therapist assumes that the client will react to her as if she were a figure from his past. Put differently, the therapist anticipates that the client will expect her to behave toward him in the same way important figures did when he was growing up.

In manifold ways each of us misperceives others in the present by bringing to bear accurate perceptions of others learned in the past. We are quite sure that certain kinds of people will behave in certain ways. So convinced are we of the accuracy of these ancient expectations that frequently we release our feelings before testing our hypotheses. Knowing how well they once functioned as protection from both real and imagined dangers, therapists work to name these still-vibrant but no longer appropriate expectations and to observe their inevitable reawakening within any progressing psychotherapy.

Psychotherapists have no concern for what is actually over; they instead attend to what from the client's past remains alive. These currently active patterns of expectation, once accurate but now no longer so, are termed "transferences."[1] Their discovery is one of the most important contributions of Sigmund Freud. Therapists hypothesize, for example, that a client who was often humiliated when growing up may lack accurate information to solve his present problems; a major reason for this lack may be his persistence in assuming, without being aware of it, that persons in his present will surely humiliate him as did persons in his past.

In most life situations we try to emphasize the determining power of external events and to minimize the effect of these ingrained expectations; in social encounters we usually ignore the latter's inappropriate consequences. During psychotherapy, by contrast, the effort is just the opposite. The therapist tries to control and minimize the effect of contemporary, external reality in order to render clear and compelling those parts of the client's current imaginings and behaviors that result from patterned expectations born in the past.

I am assuming an important and rich analogue between such misperceptions arising from our emotional histories and the misperceptions revealed when unequal parable characters reach out for one another's recognition. Alive in the imagination of each, whether in awareness or not, is more than the two persons actually face to face. They, as do we, address not only the person in front of them but also other people drawn from other times.

On entering the parable of a Widow and a Judge, we are introduced to two characters. The concept of transference, however, begins with the idea that these two characters in fact represent four. On the one hand are who the judge thinks he himself is and who the judge thinks the widow is. On the other hand, there are who the widow thinks the judge is, and who the widow thinks she herself is. These two different imaginative worlds, enclosing two different sets of patterned expectation, are built upon decades of past experience. Their foundations were settled long before the judge and the widow ever laid eyes on each other.

To explore these two different imaginative worlds, my strategy will be the same as a therapist's: (1) I will first notice who the judge thinks he himself is; I will observe in particular how his attitudes about himself affect me. (2) I will then notice who the judge thinks the widow is; I will observe how his attitudes toward her make me feel. (3) I will then assume that the judge's current attitudes and behaviors, as revealed in my feeling responses to him, reflect both the ways in which important other persons once behaved toward him and the ways he once felt about them. (My purpose throughout this effort is not to excuse the judge's behavior; my goal is to understand his imaginative world.) Such observations will lead, finally, to (4) suppositions about how the widow might understand herself and others, including the judge.[2]

Who the judge thinks he is. The judge states, "I have no fear of God and no respect for anyone." Here, I believe, is offered in compact form a perplexing series of events. On the one hand, the judge has no respect for law; on the other hand, he has spent a lifetime becoming a judge. How can one account for such an obvious contradiction? Early in his career, this man was drawn to the study of law—and thus, in the Jewish tradition, to valuing the fundamental position of God as lawgiver. Now, by rejecting any obligation to God, he is engaged in undermining the very structures he earlier embraced. How can one make sense of this transformation?

One possibility, of course, is that he has become enamored with taking bribes. Although it is indeed likely that among his current reasons for remaining a judge is some combination of greed and status, I find such an hypothesis too limited to account for the depth of his motivation. To begin with, he boasts of exercising his perfidy at the heart of the community's ability to trust. Here is sabotage of the highest order. Why is he so invested? Second, he needs to emphasize that he disdains not only tradition but other people as well. With suspect conviction he locates himself within his imaginative world as an extreme individualist. Looked at closely, he is proposing that he is totally self-originating. Why does he need to make so obviously hollow a claim?[3]

One way to approach these questions is to begin to notice how such a character makes you feel. Assuming that I am a contemporary of his, so that I myself respect aspects of our shared tradition, I begin to feel pushed aside and even insulted. I realize that what so offends me is not only his arrogance but also the completeness of his rejection. He has no regard for the people I admire; he goes so far as to account none of them as even his equal.

Then I notice that he defines himself not by what he is but by what he is not. He is not talking about an independent otherness, where he is choosing among alternatives while remaining prepared to change his point of view; instead he is manifesting an all-encompassing rejection of every outside influence. He is, I realize, refusing commerce with the rest of the world; in terms of emotional give-and-take, he claims he is neither importing nor exporting.

I then understand that his overriding purpose in life is to be in control. He keeps people at a distance when he wants and compels them to come toward him when he wants. Above all, he cannot tolerate the authority of anyone else. No third person, no law, can possibly evoke his allegiance—because then he would have to entrust control of himself to someone else.

Because he tries to be so completely in command, he appears to me to be almost completely isolated. He is bereft of just about every resource—all of which are derived from the feeling responses of others—to grasp the realities of his own inner life. He is nearly without means to discover that he is in fact the creator of his imaginative world. Only by refusing everyone access, including himself, to his own doubts and uncertainties, does he succeed in believing that he is in complete control—which, of course, he cannot possibly be.

I experience the judge's encased self-centeredness as insolent; his entitlement infuriates me. He dares represent himself as impinged upon rather than impinging. He refuses to recognize the widow's rights and then blames her when she resists. In no way would she be so persistently demanding were he not first so persistently dismissive. Yet he presumes to feel put upon!

Then I become baffled. Why does he ignore so completely the consequences of his own activity?

At this point, were I the judge's therapist, I would resist the temptation to withdraw and instead try to become curious. I might then use my two responses of anger and bafflement, together with my disgust and my desire to get away from him, to hypothesize that he once felt as this woman does and I do: angry, baffled, and rejected. Put differently, he may as an adult be mimicking the behavior of those upon whom he once depended. Just as he was earlier controlled by others and then put down for resisting that control, he now dominates this woman and blames her for his resulting distress.

Because of his focused need to attack the fundamental bases of authority, I further suppose that these early important figures lacked honesty. I see him as imposing on the widow a failed integrity that was once his lot.

Through his persistent controlling and demeaning of others, I infer that he is trying to protect himself from both sides of a lifelong dilemma: (1) what early on he perceived as the great danger of relying on anyone, and (2) his needing, like everyone else, to evoke from others a responsive recognition. He reenacts with the widow the sequence he learned to expect as a child: whenever he tried to get recognition from those on whom he depended, he was regularly shamed. To defend himself against such anticipated humiliation, he long ago determined never to depend on anyone; by never extending trust, he would never again be humiliated.

The price of such control, however, is high. The judge has lost access to all the more direct ways of gratifying his human need to depend. He has limited himself to scraping together whatever satisfaction he can from an impoverished effort to coerce what he needs.

He pays an additional price as well. Because by his disrespect his contemporaries are likely to feel put down, they are also likely to put him down. Either openly or secretly, and in spite of his eminent position, they will find ways to ridicule him. By refusing to risk respect, the judge systematically provokes the very shaming he has all his life sought to avoid.

Who the judge thinks the widow is. Although openly denying his dependency on others, secretly the judge structures his existence so as to require their presence. It is curious and wonderful to behold. With great effort he secures a public position that requires he be available to others—and then demands to be left alone! He proclaims his longing for solitude while occupying one of the few places where people must come if they are to receive their due.

Why does he not quit one side of his supposed dilemma? Why not resign his judgeship and enjoy the consequent privacy? Or why not relinquish his longing for privacy and relish the position of one who attracts the respect of the entire community? He does neither. Why? Not simply because of greed, which is a later motive nurtured by his compromises, but primarily because he seeks to maintain, out of awareness, his desire for what he disowns, namely, that he matter to another and another matter to him. With great effort he positions himself so that people must come to him, never he to them.

Into the people he then controls, he places his own unacknowledged desire for human contact. His longing for the response of another he hides from himself and puts into the woman. He imagines it is she who wants him; he does not suspect that in fact it may be he who wants her. Indeed, what strategy is better calculated to compel someone's undivided attention than to reject a person's rights while remaining the sole protector of those rights?

The judge claims that she, by her persistent badgering, is the one who is keeping their contact alive; otherwise, he implies, he would be happy to be left alone. Then why does he not use his obvious power to get rid of her? Because secretly he is depending on her; he reveals this dependency by requiring the repetitive presence he disdains.

By his account he does away with her persistence because she is wearing him out. The real reason may be, however, that he is coming uncomfortably close to realizing his hidden desire for her presence. Ironically, in this reading, he vindicates her not because she is damaging him but because he is becoming aware of wanting her.

Thus, the judge misperceives—first himself and then the other. He requires the widow's presence and then dismisses her, thereby both gratifying and discounting his hidden longings. He is caught up in an unconscious dilemma. His whole way of life, which he believes to be autonomous in the extreme, functions narrowly in a single-minded effort to compel the very dependency he dares not own.

(This reading can be expanded to assume that the judge is engaged in a sadistic voyeurism. Such an understanding would discern his motives not simply as sexual but as an attempt to extend his need for control into the sexual realm. Here he might be seen as compelling the woman's repetitive pleading because secretly he enjoys the titillation of her impassioned helplessness.)[4]

Who the widow thinks the judge is. Within the limits set by the parable, the widow has no resources beyond what the judge provides. She turns to him because she has no one else to turn to. (Such limits supply an apt metaphor for the experience of a child with its parents.)[5]

But the judge is unable to provide. His lack of empathy for himself spills over into her; any response purporting to come from him is, finally, the product of her own persistence.

How might the widow be responding to such a complete absence? No one is there; no one is with her who wants her to become someone of unique value. The judge has erased her; he imagines the widow essentially by not imagining her. Just as he structures his environment to exclude awareness of his own inner experience, so he prevents any expression of hers. How, then, does one speculate on the widow's understanding of this person who does not allow her to be?

I imagine that she perceives the judge as one might a dictator who has always controlled every source of information. She is tempted to assume, in spite of all her efforts not to, that somehow his attitudes and behavior toward her are appropriate.

Who the widow thinks she herself is. While the judge appears engrossed in his own self-deception, the widow seems nearly suffocated by his definitions. By virtue of her weak standing in the community, she is almost without resources to counter the judge's desire to erase her. She is forced again and again to appeal to this man for recognition and then forced again and again to submit to his excited indifference. She is enveloped in his inner deadness while trying to keep alive her right for a response she is almost certain she will never receive.

The widow is so surrounded and covered by the judge's seeming indifference that it is hard to imagine her apart from his consuming presence. Since in their joint world there is no law, no third authority outside the two of them to require him to live up to his obligations, her single option is the counter-control of stubbornness; by such a strategy she succeeds for a time in frustrating his complete dominance. (Although he can manage any form of bribery, seduction, or cowed withdrawal, he is baffled by her demand that he be the one to change.)

But she has no resources to counterattack. As with a person invaded by a toxic infection, she must devote all of her energy to surviving. In particular, she is not free to discover how she might, on her own terms, exercise an autonomous assertiveness. Indeed, she may well lose any opportunity to experiment with her own independent strivings. Two options may be the only ones left her: First, she may become depressed, that is, attack herself. Then, in the recesses of her constant self-accusations ("I am unworthy; I cannot be loved."), one may discern, still alive, the outlines of the judge's disowned self-doubt.

Second, she may become abusive. Were she at some point to gain access to a form of power at all similar to that of the judge, the shape of her suppressed aggression might at last be discovered. Because she has for so long been compelled to live in response to imposed definitions, she might reveal herself eventually as so defined. Having been humiliated, she may, in the end, become one who humiliates.[6]

The judge's dilemma is out of his awareness; that of the widow remains voiceless. Only the listener is free to wrestle with the origins and consequences of both.

Using "Projective Identification" to Understand Alien Worlds

This section offers the second of two ways of listening given to psychotherapists that may be of use to parable listeners: therapists hypothesize that long-standing patterns of expectation imposed on the present by one partner sometimes fit together with and support very different patterns of expectation imposed by the other.

An example of this hypothesis is found in a not uncommon form of marriage.[7] In this relationship two different patterns of expectation, arising out of two different personal histories, fit together and become mutually supportive.

A wife, for example, might not be concerned about her passive longings but anticipates feeling guilty about her potentially destructive aggression. Her husband has no conflict about his aggression but expects to feel shame about his need to depend. These two contrasting persons seek each other out. They do so because the long-standing pattern of expectation of the first fits with and supports the very different pattern of expectation of the second. Expecting to be destructive, the wife disowns her aggression. Instead she vicariously experiences that dangerous aggression in her husband, unconsciously encourages him in it, and consciously disdains him for it. In parallel fashion, the husband, expecting to be humiliated, disowns his dependency. Instead he vicariously experiences that feared dependency in his wife, unconsciously encourages her in it, and consciously disdains her for it. The resulting dysfunction is difficult to resolve because each partner finds, in the other's blameworthy behavior, unconscious gratification.

What follows is a working out for the parable of Tenant Farmers and a Landlord various possibilities uncovered by this idea of two separate patterns of maladaptive expectation fitting together and—tragically—becoming mutually supportive. In psychoanalytic terminology, this constellation is termed "projective identification." It can be broken down into four basic steps, listed below, with comments on the parable following each step.[8] These steps represent the development of an increasingly rigidified set of mistaken certainties, built on earlier misunderstandings, in turn fostered by even earlier misperceptions.

First, we deny the existence of an uncomfortable aspect of ourselves and we disown the fact that we want to be that way:

•The tenants disown their powerlessness.

•The landlord disowns his power.

Outside of their awareness and for their own reasons, the tenants feel ashamed of their subordinate position. Unconsciously they disown their powerlessness and instead place this hated attribute into the landlord.

Outside of his awareness and for his own reasons, the landlord, "a good man," feels guilty about being dominant. Unconsciously disowning the fact of his power, he fails to suppose the obvious, namely, that he has engaged his tenants in a contract that at least some of them perceive as unjust.

Second, we discover another person who already possesses, for his or her separate reasons, that aspect of ourselves we want to disown. That other person in turn then lets us "have" (or participate in) the disowned aspect of ourselves as part of himself or herself:

•The tenants appear (for a time) powerful.

•The landlord appears (for a time) powerless.

The tenants already tend toward being aggressive; their world is one of rebellious assertiveness. They are quite certain the exercise of raw power will be both necessary and successful.

The landlord already tends toward being compliant; his world is one of obedience to law. He does not at all anticipate, nor is he at all comfortable with, having to exercise raw power.

Third, we identify the other person (now seen as possessing the disowned characteristic) as unlike ourselves and therefore disdain him or her, while at the same time we maintain the relationship in such a way that we continue to experience vicariously the disowned attribute:

•Discovering their disowned powerlessness in the landlord, the tenants repeatedly go against major pieces of evidence and humiliate him; disdain in them is rife.

•Because he himself so completely disowns it, the landlord goes against major pieces of evidence and dismisses the possibility that his tenants could become powerful; disdain in him is rife.

The tenants disdain the landlord's "weakness." Their complete confidence he will not retaliate is based on their having placed into him their own unconscious conviction that they in fact are the ones who are weak. So certain are they of the landlord's weakness, they confidently behave so as to render the landlord, for a time at least, to appear weak. They refuse to speak; they refuse to lay out demands; they refuse to negotiate. Instead, they continue to wound and humiliate the landlord's representatives.

The landlord, in turn, for his own unconscious reasons, actually enacts the tenants' expectations. After receiving back his first wounded slave, he neither demands an explanation nor provides his next representative with enough power to enforce compliance. Certain that his tenants are as submissive to law as he is, he fails to suspect that a lethal rebellion is brewing. To these tenants, then, he indeed appears as if he will let them have their way. (Here may be part of the parable's tragedy. Had the landlord been firmer at the beginning of the story, he might have avoided not only his loss but, after the story ends, his own likely murderousness.)

Fourth and finally, participants do not attend to any of the real aspects of the other person that may contradict the placing of the disowned attribute into the other:

•The tenants steadfastly refuse to imagine that the landlord might become powerful.

•The landlord steadfastly refuses to imagine that the tenants might feel resentment.

The tenants mistakenly evaluate as powerlessness the landlord's mistaken assumption that they have failed to recognize his representatives as from him. The tenants know that to rough up the owner's slave is tantamount to roughing up the landlord himself. But they refuse to anticipate that they are in any danger. If queried, they might observe that the landlord could retaliate. But deep down they know he will not. They do not respect, for their own unconscious reasons, the possibility that the landlord will counter their aggression with an equal aggression of his own. Because of their prior need to deny and place in the landlord their own weakness, they know for a certainty the "fact" that the landlord will remain weak.

The landlord, in his turn, refuses to see the evidence of resentment written on the bloodied bodies of his emissaries. He insists, good man that he is, that they see the world of superiors and subordinates to be as lawful and just as he does. Thus, he will go on believing that his subordinates willingly and with dignity entered into their contract with him. Thus, he will misdiagnose his wounded slaves as cases of mistaken identity rather than as the harbingers of an enraged rebellion. Thus, the story builds toward an intense irony. The landlord is responding as if the problem is one of recognition—of himself. The tenants are responding as if the problem is one of recognition—of themselves.

The landlord says to his increasingly anxious companions: "Why should those farmers have any complaint? Why, they are just like me: good men who obey the law! How could they possibly have any disagreement with me? Just as I submit to the law that holds these arrangements together, so do they. Everything has been agreed to. It's only a misunderstanding. You'll see." The tenants, in their turn, say to each other, "The only way to stick it to this bastard is to raise the stakes."

These totally contrasting but complementary certainties, simultaneously fixed within landlord and tenants, together become a major clue alerting the listener that what psychotherapists call "projective identification," as outlined in the steps above, is taking place. This clue may be recognized by the utter bewilderment it produces in the observer.

For the listener, unlike either parable participant, has been growing more and more restless.

To the tenants the listener protests with mounting anxiety, "What are you doing? Isn't it obvious what will happen to you if you keep on wounding this man's slaves?" The listener expects that the landlord will at least demand restitution or, more likely, will retaliate with force. It is the listener, not the tenants, who is amazed by the appearance of yet another defenseless messenger on the horizon. And it is the listener whose questions border on the incoherent when finally the landlord's unprotected son approaches the vineyard: "How can you risk your son? How can you be so stupid? Who are you, failing to conserve what is yours and now endangering what is most precious to you? Are you mad?"[9]

The process becomes increasingly out of control. First, the landlord's disowning of his dominance fuels the tenants' inarticulate rebellion. Then the landlord's incomprehensible tolerance fans its flames. Both parties collude in sliding toward an increasing reliance on unmodulated power. By not responding with firmness, the landlord both fails to protect what is his and frustrates his tenants' distorted efforts to claim recognition.

The irony and its tragedy intensify. Those unable to recognize the father's slaves immediately recognize the father's son. Failing to make the father see, they trace all too clearly where his eye falls. There, unforeseen, they strike. The gleam in the father's eye dies and with it, in an awful spasm, the tenants also die. All that remains is wasteland.

The Listener as Passive Recipient or Authoritative Observer

These two parables at the outset seem like the judge: unresponsive to probing and resistant to resolution. Yet in spite of their opaqueness—or because of it—these stories still draw one in. Both raise and seem not to answer the question of how one gains the confidence to wonder what is really going on. How does the listener move from being a bewildered recipient of their mystery to becoming an authoritative observer of their complexity?

Because no such observer is available within either story, an endless cycle of oppression there ensues. Each protagonist is limited to laying vigorous claim upon the other to do the right thing. By the other's agreeing to self-denigration, she or he is to render the first one's imaginative world complete. Either the widow must submit so as to make the judge complete on his terms, or the judge must submit so as to make the widow complete on hers. Either the landlord must submit so as to render the tenants complete on their terms, or the tenants must submit so as to render the landlord complete on his.

Not only is law absent; lacking also is anyone who can describe what is really going on. Each lays his or her demands on the other because no third is present to enable each to wonder. No one exists even to hold together the beginning articulations of their differing points of view—so that the participants might together discern what the trouble is and themselves become able to bring about change.

The role of a balanced observer, so completely vacated within the parables themselves, falls to the listener. If, however, we do not grasp the range of misperceptions among the characters, we too may be tempted to sustain their seemingly irreconcilable differences. We do so by not including conflicting data. Instead we turn away from the complexity of inclusiveness and tend to split our experience of the characters into "bad" and "good." Within this stance, we examine and condemn one character and ignore and idealize the other.

From a psychotherapeutic point of view, such a parceling out of condemnation and idealization represents resistance to a more differentiated grasp of human experience. From an observer point of view, such a strategy leads to a loss of listener confidence in being able to discern what is really going on; behavior remains mysterious and the listener becomes bewildered.

A major alternative is to look closely at both sides. Such a transition within the listener, so that she or he implicates both characters as sources of misunderstanding, is a hard one to make—partly because it positions one better to observe one's own misperceptions. Nonetheless, I believe that such a shift toward focused evenhandedness is not only vital to resolving the parable's tensions; in the difficult work of observing what is happening, it becomes essential to the growth of a listener's sense of authority.

Listener difficulty in implicating both parable protagonists as sources of misperception increases exponentially when we turn to our next parable. Here, in the Prodigal Son, is encountered the august person of the forgiving father, a character so widely accepted as among the greatest exemplars of nonretaliatory love as to appear blameless.

6

A Younger Son and a Father

Among the parables attributed to Jesus, the Prodigal Son is by far the most complex. Beyond the reaches of its extensive commentary there remain, I believe, important regions of the narrative's complexity yet to be explored. My own perspectives, which range at a distance from established positions, took their start from insights provided by James Breech.[1]

I will discuss the second part of this parable, here renamed Two Sons and a Father, in chapter 7. Its first part, which I am calling a Younger Son and a Father, reads as follows:

The Situation
There was a man who had two sons.

Scene 1
The younger of them said to his father, "Father, give me the share of the property that will belong to me." So he divided his property between them.

Scene 2
A few days later the younger son gathered all he had and traveled to a distant country, and there he squandered his property in dissolute living. When he had spent everything, a severe famine took place throughout that country, and he began to be in need. So he went and hired himself out to one of the citizens of that country, who sent him to his fields to feed the pigs. He would gladly have

*filled himself with the pods that the pigs were eating; and no one
gave him anything. But when he came to himself he said, "How
many of my father's hired hands have bread enough and to spare,
but here I am dying of hunger! I will get up and go to my father,
and I will say to him, 'Father, I have sinned against heaven and
before you; I am no longer worthy to be called your son; treat me
like one of your hired hands.' " So he set off and went to his father.*

Scene 3

*But while he was still far off, his father saw him and was filled with
compassion; he ran and put his arms around him and kissed him.
The son said to him, "Father, I have sinned against heaven and
before you; I am no longer worthy to be called your son." But the
father said to his slaves, "Quickly, bring out a robe—the best
one—and put it on him; put a ring on his finger and sandals on his
feet. And get the fatted calf and kill it, and let us eat and celebrate;
for this son of mine was dead and is alive again; he was lost and is
found!" And they began to celebrate. (Luke 15: 11b-24)*

With a simple and revolutionary proposition, James Breech has
opened a gateway into novel possibilities for this story. Once this proposition is entertained, the options available to the listener are considerably
enlarged.

Nearly all English-speaking commentators perceive in the father of
this parable a figure for God. As a consequence, almost no one probes
the significance of this man's decision, while still alive and capable, to
relinquish control over his estate to his two sons. Sometimes he is
described as generous, sometimes as foolish. But most often, almost consistently, the implications of this extraordinary act are not explored.

For Breech, however, the father's willingness to comply with his
younger son's request is so unusual that it calls for careful inquiry.

The father has given in to his younger son's demand, contrary to
expectation. To do so, he had to overlook, or to ignore, the fact that
the younger son was attempting to manipulate him, and that the
younger son was treating him as though already dead. The man inexplicably does even more than demanded. He divides his entire living

between his two sons, giving the part demanded to his younger son and the rest, unasked for, to his elder son. If the man had simply given his younger son what he demanded, the listener could conclude that the man was under the spell of his younger son.

The man's action of dividing his living between his sons creates a situation the significance of which must be clearly understood. In the thinking of the ancient world, questions regarding ownership of property and questions regarding father-son relationships were inextricable. What the man does—allowing himself to be treated as though dead and giving away his proprietary rights—is utterly unparalleled in any of the parabolic narratives which survive from antiquity (Jewish, Greek, or Latin). Since the situation is so extraordinary, the narrative raises the question of why the man, by dividing his living between his two sons, totally altered the basis of his relationship with them.[2]

Why indeed? I believe any full reading of this parable must attempt to answer Breech's question.

Parental Giving or Parental Depriving?

There was a man who had two sons. The younger of them said to his father, "Father, give me the share of the property that will belong to me." So he divided his property between them.

Commentators before Breech had already observed that the younger son's request implies a wish that his father die.[3] Bailey writes:

For over fifteen years I have been asking people of all walks of life from Morocco to India and from Turkey to the Sudan about the implications of a son's request for his inheritance while the father is living. The answer has almost always been emphatically the same. . . . The conversation runs as follows:
  "Has anyone ever made such a request in your village?"
  "Never!"
  "Could anyone ever make a request?"
  "Impossible!'
  "If anyone ever did, what would happen?"
  "His father would beat him, of course!"

"Why?"

"The request means—he wants his father to die!"[4]

Some observers of the father's action quote from the apocryphal book of Ecclesiasticus, also called The Wisdom of Jesus Son of Sirach:

> As long as you live, give no power over yourself—son or wife, brother or friend. Do not give your property to another, in case you change your mind and want it back. As long as you have life and breath, never change places with anyone. It is better for your children to ask from you than for you to be dependent on them. Whatever you are doing, keep the upper hand, and allow no blot on your reputation. Let your life run its course, and then, at the hour of death distribute your estate. (Ecclesiasticus 33: 19-23, NEB)

In Shakespeare's *King Lear,* after Lear, ignoring Kent's warnings, has divided his kingdom among his daughters, a subplot develops. In it the bastard Edmund by a ruse seeks to turn his father Gloucester against his legitimate brother Edgar, saying, "I have heard him oft maintain it to be fit that, sons at perfect age and fathers declined, the father should be as ward to the son, and the son manage his revenue."

To this supposed desire by a son to control the father's estate while the latter still lives, Gloucester's response is instant and unequivocal:

> "O villain, villain! His very opinion in the letter! Abhorred villain! Unnatural, detested, brutish villain! worse than brutish! Go, sirrah, seek him; I'll apprehend him. Abominable villain! Where is he?"[5]

A different but equally aroused response by a father to his son's premature grasping for paternal prerogatives is provided by a near contemporary of Jesus, the great Augustan poet Ovid. Phaethon, come to Apollo to claim recognition of his lineage as born to the god by the nymph Clymene, draws this rash promise from his father:

> "O well worthy to be owned my son. . . .
> To still all question, ask what boon thou wilt—
> Ere asked I grant thee.
> By Styx, dread oath of Gods. . . .
> I swear."

Phaethon, in the heat of adolescent grandiosity, demands for a day to drive his father's sun-bearing chariot across the heavens. Apollo, trapped in his oath, is overwrought:

> "Bethink thee, O my son, nor let thy sire
> With fatal gift undo thee! While thou mayest,
> Amend thy suit. Thou wouldst by certain proof
> Assure thy parentage. My grief supplies
> The pledge—thy father's fears the father prove.
> Look on me! Would thy glance my inmost heart
> Could penetrate, and read the sire within!
> Oh! ransack all the treasures of the world,
> Earth, sea and sky—choose what thou wilt of all
> Their gifts, nor dread denial! This alone
> Forbear to see,—false honor,—certain bane!
> The boon thou seekest is thy doom, my son!"[6]

In marked contrast to these examples of paternal resistance to a son's premature reach for paternal authority, the father of this parable, toward a manifestly immature son, offers no resistance at all.

One specialist in ancient Palestinian legal affairs estimates that the younger son, who is most likely unmarried and about seventeen, receives two-ninths of his father's property, resigns any right to participate in the estate at his father's death, but remains obligated by custom and religious law to support his father until he dies. The father, in turn, signs over the remainder of his property to his elder son, using the formula "from today and after my death."

> By means of this formula he gave the [elder son] no right to possession as he gave the younger—who could proceed to demand partition and arrange an auction if necessary . . . but a right to succeed at the father's death and to question meanwhile all alienation including gifts which were outside the father-donor's legal powers.[7]

Here, awaiting the listener at the very beginning, is a major gap in the parable. What does the father believe he has provided by relinquishing control over his own resources? What does he imagine his younger son will experience when he deeds over to him most of his stocks and fine art, two of the cars, and the summer cottage? What has the younger son really requested? What does he believe he has in fact received?

Many observe the multiple meanings of the Greek word for what the father gives: *bios,* that is, "means of subsistence," "property," "manner of life conduct" or, literally, "life." Some commentators, as already noted, have discerned in the younger son's demand a wish for his father's death. But none has supposed that the father's compliance may represent, in reciprocal fashion, an attack upon his son's developing life.

Can the father in fact give of himself in such a self-sacrificing, premature, and conclusive manner without inflicting great damage? Can parents while still competent relinquish control over their resources without at the same time communicating to the next generation serious doubt about the latter's ability to discover their own? By preempting the risks each child must take to become adults, the father may be seducing each to remain a child.

The matter may be even more complex. Here may be represented not only the father's loss of confidence in his children's capacity to develop but also a loss of confidence in himself. By divesting himself prematurely, he may be pressing upon his sons the awesome possibility that their father's life purposes have become empty of meaning. They may apprehend, with growing anxiety, that their father now looks to them to supply that meaning. Because he seems to abandon his work, his children may feel obligated to complete it.

What makes the father's behavior so confusing is that it occurs in a context of nurturing. It is not easy to suppose that this giving, generous, and caring man may in fact be dangerously encouraging aspects of his sons' infantile life. The unconditional acceptance essential to earlier stages of development, if left unbalanced at later stages by a confident limit-setting, can lead to substantial dilemmas. The moment the father provides the inheritance, he may be withholding what his sons most need: the father's confidence in the ongoing significance of his own life's work coupled with a sure expectation of his sons' independent growth.

Masud Khan, a psychoanalyst, has conceptualized the consequences of parental failure to represent limits. About the seriously overgratified child he writes:

The infancy and childhood of these patients are characterized by an over-protective environment that precipitately anticipated and met the needs of the child and coped with them in an almost magically effective way. This type of environmental care of the infant child does not allow any room for aggressive behavior, which is essential to the crystallization of identity and separateness of selfhood in the child. . . . What is split off from experiential reality [in these children] is the whole range of aggressive behavior patterns and capacities. This leads to a lack of initiative and confidence that aggressive confrontation with anyone will be less than disastrous and catastrophic to their person . . . as well as the [other]. The intense idealization of the infant child and over-saturated care of his nascent needs lead him to internalize an idolized image of himself, which is henceforth his most dynamic internal object. . . . Hence in all later situations such children are trapped in a paradoxical stalemate: they crave to refind this early model of magical care and dependence, and yet must not surrender to it because it entails annihilation of all possibilities of discovering their own initiative and aggressive potential in their own person.[8]

How will late adolescent or young adult children respond if parents draw them away from the disciplined conditions of adult growth and back toward the limitless nurturance of infantile dependency? How will they manage their reawakened ambivalence about that earlier paradise for which they will always yearn but nonetheless must forever renounce?

Peter Blos, reputed for his psychoanalytic work with adolescents, captures Greek mythology's understanding of this central adolescent conflict—one that the father, by his generosity, may be seriously disrupting:

We are well acquainted with the proverbial crossroads at which the adolescent finds himself. The reference to "crossroads" in this context should remind the reader of the spot on which Oedipus, traveling to Thebes, entered into mortal combat with Laius, his father, whose carriage stubbornly blocked the son's way. . . . The contest and clash of wills, as told in the Oedipus myth, reflects in paradigmatic essence the universal crisis of the adolescent boy: two sets of enticements and urges are beckoning him in opposite directions. They are those of emotional retreat to earlier childhood positions, when parental idealizations rendered life dependable and predictable, and those of aggressive self-determination and independence, leading into the unknown and unpredictable future.[9]

Blos elsewhere writes:

> We must remember that every boy once—fleetingly or more lastingly—
> identified with the role of the envied and admired procreative woman:
> the mother. I have observed how these trends in the small boy become
> pathologically aggravated when his father, disillusioned in his conjugal
> life, shifts his need for emotional fulfillment from his wife to his son.
> Whenever I hear a father say in the consultation preceding the treat-
> ment of his son, "The only one I love in this world is my son," I feel
> alerted to the central complex of the patient.[10]

In the present narrative both children, in order to nourish their
father—and, perhaps, to retain the securities such regressive strategies
supply—may be tempted to betray their own becoming; both may fear
their success will subject their father to failure. Indeed, both seem to
resolve this conflict by choosing deprivation. The younger engineers a
separation that by unconscious design leads to a resourceless dependency. (The elder, whose dilemmas will be described in the following
chapter, flees in the opposite direction, into compliance. Yet he too, like
his wayward brother, seems determined to discover himself resourceless.)
By his gift-giving in the absence of confident limit-setting, the father may
be depriving his growing sons of a father who deprives.[11]

The Listener's Choosing

Parable listeners do not often observe their own listening. As they reach
this point, many are unaware that they have just entered a major gap or
unexplained sequence in this narrative and that they are now called upon
to select one from a wide array of possible alternatives to make sense of
it. After the younger son receives his inheritance, listeners must decide:
(1) how the son now sees his father, (2) how the son now sees himself,
and (3) what feelings he now has.

Listed below are some of the alternatives available when trying to
imagine how the younger son responds to his father's effort to provide
him present control over a future he must yet discover. Listeners may
assume that he experiences no ambivalence at all:

1. He perceives his father as loving and generous.

2. He feels freed of familial restraints; he is confident he will be able to manage his future successfully.

3. He is grateful to his father for this evidence of trust in him; as he travels to a far country he is feeling optimistic about his future.

Or, listeners may believe he is slightly ambivalent:

1. He perceives the father as generous but not fully aware. He is vaguely puzzled why his father did not insist that his competencies are as yet incompletely developed. Nonetheless, relinquishing his own uncertainty in the matter, he accepts his father's perspective and decides to plunge forward.

2. The son wants to believe he is autonomous. He quickly dismisses any doubts he might have about his capacity to replace the supports of his family. He resists thinking about his future; he is out to have a good time.

3. He spends his inheritance with a sense of carefree power; he is fascinated with the control over others his money provides.

Or, listeners may decide he is more acutely ambivalent:

1. He had been feeling increasingly smothered by his father's continuing insistence that he, the father, provide everything for him. After receiving the inheritance the son had for a brief time felt gloriously free. But now, in moments between periods of elation, he is aware of a disappointment he struggles to identify. In making his demand for the inheritance he had with ambivalence been hoping his father would refuse and instead firmly encourage him to develop more of his own resources.

2. Without knowing why, he believes he must flee; he must act urgently, make a total break, and not look back.

3. In general he feels energized by an excitement he can neither name nor control. However, when alone with himself—an experience he mostly avoids—he sometimes feels terrified.

The following pages explore the coherence of what may be discovered by pursuing portions of the third option described above. As with any developing interpretation, the reader may evaluate how well the following descriptions fit together the spoken and unspoken parts of this story.

Separation and Boundaries

The younger said to his father, "Give me. . . ."

The son does not approach his father tentatively and with a question, but imperiously and with a demand. I assume that the arrogance of his challenge is in direct proportion to his out-of-awareness fear that he might succeed. He is unconsciously afraid that his father will fail to maintain those generational boundaries he must experience if he is to grow.

I believe the son does not truly want his father's property. His seemingly hurtful demand that the father treat himself as if dead, in fact, represents his ambivalent but hopeful longing that his parent come alive, reveal himself as father, and assume an authority over the limits of reality that for a long time has been missing. The son reaches for his father's property in an attempt to reach his father's limits. His pushing into his father is an effort to push against those boundaries necessary between the generations; the son wants assurance that his father will insist on completing the work that is his, thus revealing the father's confidence that the son in time will accomplish the work belonging to himself.

But when the father agrees to supply his son so completely from within his own living, the son understands that his father has concluded that he, the son, is incapable of any separate living. He discerns, hidden within the father's largess, the latter's conviction that he himself possesses nothing of substance on which to build.

In order to have his father, the son must persist in wanting. But in wanting what? He cannot distinguish what the father wants for him from what the father needs from him; these separate desires appear to him to merge. Whether in awareness or not, the son begins to entertain an awesome possibility: to maintain his father's life he may have to obliterate his own. He then grasps at straws; the only way out is to flee—or to destroy what he cannot flee.

Once the younger son takes possession of his inheritance, he reveals a conviction that he is empty; in his subsequent behavior he displays no resources to create but only a readiness to consume. As his father seems to do, the son demonstrates an incapacity to imagine a future with himself in it. The son's destruction of the father's provision, like the father's giving itself, is mindless of what is to come. He becomes intent, rather, on rendering useless that which he can find no way to use. Lacking paternal presence, he will lay waste to the signifiers of paternal absence.

I understand the son's reprehensible profligacy as a despairing throwing away of useless paternal resources. The son's squandering of his father's provision becomes a mirror image of the father's squandering of his position as father.

Somewhere the son knows that his present entitlement is a false echo of a forever ended infancy. Somehow he knows that he cannot stand . . . being indulged. In this light, the young man's squandering appears as his grandiose, then desperate, and finally humiliating effort to tell the truth.

This truth is that the father is using his still dependent son to fulfill his own need to be needed. In giving the inheritance, the father withholds both the son's chance to discover, and the father's chance to recognize, the son's own capacities to create. By enabling his son to leave prematurely, the father has rendered inevitable his eventual return.

Separation and Regression

The younger son . . . traveled to a distant country, and there he squandered his property in dissolute living.

At some level the son understands, even before he leaves, that he will have to return. Somehow he knows that not only can he make no use of the largess his father provides, he must also relinquish what remains of his resources. To keep his father, he must defeat himself. To ensure the realization of this unconscious certainty, the son complements his father's divestment by throwing away everything beyond the inheritance that might otherwise have supported his efforts at autonomy: ties with family, friends, country, and religion.

The son wants to separate from his father. Perhaps he believes that he is about to be on his own. Certainly he uses his inheritance to engineer the illusion of control. But what does he in fact do? In going to a distant country, he goes straight back to "infantile dependencies, grandiosities, safeties, and gratifications."[12]

Vividly missing in his new world is any sense of limit. He cannot tolerate the least form of delay. He is all present tense. The father's absence appears most clearly in the son's inability to anticipate; one is astonished at how quickly he dissipates his resources among strangers. He manifests the child's intolerance of having his self-image subjected to the stringencies of his social surround.[13] He grasps again the illusion that he can have whatever he wants when he wants it. In fleeing to a far country, he has returned to his childhood.

By such an immediate—although certainly disguised and symbolic—regression to the center of his early family, the son is attempting, I believe, to do two things: he is trying to dramatize his unacknowledged deprivation and at the same time restore what he has lost.

By rejecting limits, he may be proclaiming his conviction that he has lost the father of his adolescence—and has thereby lost his way. He cannot move forward because the father he seeks is behind him. His carelessness toward his future reflects his father's intolerance of a son who will not remain a child. By staging a short-lived reenactment of that childhood, the son may be trying to say, in the only way he knows how, that he is bereft of the discipline necessary to become an adult; all that is left to him is the limitless nurturance of infancy.[14]

By squandering the son is also trying to imitate—and thereby possess—the parent he has lost. When he spends recklessly and without forethought, he is doing exactly what his father did. As his father tried to keep his son by giving away his resources, so the son will do the same; by becoming like his father, he will attempt to keep the only father he has.

Separation and Fragmentation

When [the younger son] had spent everything, a severe famine took place throughout that country, and he began to be in need. So he went and hired himself out to one of the citizens of that country, who sent him to his fields to feed the pigs. He would gladly have filled himself with the pods that the pigs were eating; and no one gave him anything.

Psychoanalytic theory proposes that when a developmental need is seriously prevented, that failure is often too painful to be experienced directly. Instead, the one who suffers it expresses that intolerable reality through unclear and fragmented means.[15]

The son has put out of awareness his frustrated longing for his father's limit-setting; this loss is too painful for him to describe. Instead, he represents his ongoing need by breaking it up into pieces. One fragment has already been described: failing to discover limits at home, the son engages in the destruction of limits abroad.

Now a second, equally disguised fragment appears. In a far country and at a far extreme of need, the son encounters a much-distorted version of that same limit which, in the center of his family, he could not find. Struggling as long as possible to escape a father who feeds but does not demand, the son at last backs into a "father" who demands but does not feed. By finally reaching both the inexorable limit of hunger and the unremitting stinginess of the owner of pigs, the son dramatizes, in superlatives, his need to be freed from being fed.

Substantial irony may reside in this moment. Breech has described the son's condition in the following terms: "The younger son could not take care of anyone, not even himself. His situation had become so desperate that he had to attach himself to someone else even to survive."[16] However, what if the son's actions in that distant country accurately reflect the father's actions inside his family? Thus: "The [father] could not take care of anyone, not even himself. His situation had become so desperate that [the father] had to attach himself to [his sons] even to survive."

Rescue or Repetition?

But when he came to himself he said, How many of my father's hired hands have bread enough and to spare, but here I am dying of hunger! I will get up and go to my father, and I will say to him, "Father, I have sinned before heaven and against you; I am no longer worthy to be called your son; treat me like one of your hired hands." So he set off and went to his father.

The younger son comes to himself not when he is impoverished but when he reaches the outer limit of hunger. Pushing at last against that wall, he can now be certain he has no choice but to return. Throughout this entire sequence the son has unconsciously striven to reach this point; he has steadily and systematically destroyed every resource other than his father. Now, finally freed from his own becoming, he can place himself once again in the gun-sights of his father's need to be needed. Now he may be helplessly confident that he has no alternative than to save his father by submitting to his father's saving sustenance.

The son's actual confession may hide a deeper guilt. He consciously acknowledges his responsibility for squandering the patrimony and thus failing in his filial obligation to support his father. But he may also be responding to a larger crime, that of having aspired to grow into adulthood. His unconscious determination not to survive after leaving his father may in fact represent his guilt for ever having wanted to do so in the first place.

In the world of this father and this son, should the son truly succeed in leaving home—that is, become a man—the father might not survive. Were he to have prospered in that distant country, the son's competence would have doomed him to live in a parentless world; he would have betrayed a father who was depending on his son's dependency to maintain his own well-being.

The son renders himself incompetent in order to preserve the only father he has ever known—the one who perceives in his children's separate abilities the harbinger of intolerable loss. The son cannot risk giving up his devotion to his father's need to be needed. Now, at this moment in the story, he has succeeded in restoring his position as a dependent child. Now, as he turns back to where the father provides and the son receives, the son once again fulfills his filial obligation by enabling his father to thrive.

The son's defeat, therefore, may be a form of victory. By securing blame for himself, the son rescues his father. So intolerable, however, is the cost of this victory that he must render his rescue unconsciously. Having paid for his father's life with the loss of his own, he remains, on his return, unaware of the full dimensions of his love and hate. He is aware only of an imprecise and unpersuasive sense of guilt.

Many commentators observe that the son wants merely to be fed. But they do not develop the implications of the son's propensity to imagine "food" when he thinks of "father." The son conceives of his father as one who feeds because he has never known his father to do otherwise. He imagines "food" when he thinks of "father" because he has always experienced his father not as one who promotes autonomy but only as one who provides sustenance.

Nonetheless, the son makes one last effort to elicit what he needs. At this point he stops thinking either of his father's feelings or of his father's desires. Instead, he imagines his father's hired hands. He focuses not only on his father feeding these people but also on his father hiring them. He conjures that part of his father who, with his employees, *both* feeds *and* demands. He imagines persons with whom the father enters into contract, whom the father pays for work provided. Here, perhaps, might be a way out. If he could achieve the status of one who, as a hired hand, must work in order to be fed, he might escape the impoverishment of one who, as a son, must consume in order to save.

There may be considerable irony in the son's soliloquy, "How many of my father's hired hands have bread enough and to spare, but here I am dying of hunger!" The hired hands may indeed be better off than he, his father's child, not because he feeds them but because the father expects significant work from them. The father's unconditional giving within his family, which in the son's childhood was vital to his development, has in the context of his emerging adulthood become a danger as threatening as starvation. Could it be then, when the son tries to tell his father to "treat me like one of your hired hands," he is making one final effort to transform his father into a father, that is, into one who makes demands upon him?

The retreat of the father as father in the son's experience forms the prelude to the father's coming presence. As the father emerges into prominence, the son recedes into childhood.

Exclusion Hidden within Inclusion

But while [the younger son] was still far off, his father saw him and was filled with compassion; he ran and put his arms around him and kissed him. Then the son said to him, "Father, I have sinned against heaven and before you; I am no longer worthy to be called your son."

But the father said to his slaves, "Quickly, bring out a robe—the best one—and put it on him; put a ring on his finger and sandals on his feet. And get the fatted calf and kill it, and let us eat and cele-

brate, for this son of mine is dead and is found again; he was lost and is found!" And they began to celebrate.

On his return the son discovers not limit but nurturance. The father runs and kisses. "This son of mine," he says, "was dead and is alive again." Alive for whom? For the son? Or for a father who needs this young adult to remain a receptive child?[17]

Scott develops an observation initiated by the Entrevernes Group, namely, that the father has become like the mother of a much younger child: "To kiss affectionately hints at the maternal theme. . . . The father's . . . response indicates that he will not follow legal or paternal roles; he will play the nourishing role."[18] The crucial issue here is not that the father functions at a level more appropriate to earlier life stages but that in so doing he fails to exercise that portion of the role required of any parent of an adolescent, namely, to represent the limits of reality.

Is the younger son undergoing rehabilitation or is he once again being deprived of those very limits he must encounter if he is to grow? The parable introduces a reconciliation that can be understood as either fundamentally true or fundamentally false. I perceive the latter, because the underlying reasons for the son's destroying the patrimony have not been addressed.

Both son and father avoid that dialogue essential to any true repairing of the damage; the son avoids through inaccurate confession and the father through inaccurate forgiveness. The son does not even get into words his urgent need: "I cannot relate to you as the child you want; for God's sake, make me work like one of your hired hands!"

When father and son embrace, nothing in their relationship has changed. Earlier the son was burdened by his father's inheritance; now he is weighed down by his father's robe and ring. As he was earlier controlled by provision, now he is trapped by guilt.

I understand the father's generous moves toward reconciliation as an over-responsive effort to avoid his own guilt; he is guilty for having enticed his son to gratify his need to be an all-giving father. Having earlier placed this guilt into his son, the father, by leaving it there, now further undermines his son's collapsing autonomy.

In this reading, the return of the prodigal becomes among the most tragic of stories. There is no room in this household for two adults—only for two prodigals.

One knows that the father is not going to treat the son as a hired hand. One knows the son is going to remain submissive to the father's terrible largess. The father is not going to focus on what the son wants; the father will persist in using his son for his own needs. "This son of mine. . . ."

As things stand, neither person will change. The son will continue with devotion to agree to self-destruction. The father will continue to smile down upon the inexpressible loneliness of a son who must forever remain his child.

To those listeners prepared to entertain their larger ambiguities, I believe that these parables entrust the actual work of imagining their resolution.[19] If you sense the possibility of deprivation hidden within generosity, of exclusion lurking within inclusion, then you discover yourself in difficulty. Within the constraints of this story, and within the limits of its many contemporary analogues, you now reach the threshold of imagining how one might intervene to achieve a more adequate reconciliation. How indeed?

7

An Elder Son and a Father and Laborers and a Landowner

The second half of Two Sons and a Father (the part about the elder son) is here placed side by side with the parable of The Vineyard Workers (now given the more inclusive title of Laborers and a Landowner). The reasons for this juxtaposition will become apparent below.

The two accounts read as follows:

The Situation

There was a man who had two sons.	*A landowner . . . went out early in the morning to hire laborers for his vineyard.*

Scene 1

The younger of them said to his father, "Father, give me the share of the property that will belong to me." So he divided his property between them. . . .	*After agreeing with the laborers for the usual daily wage, he sent them into his vineyard. When he went out about nine o'clock, he saw others standing idle in the marketplace; and he said to them, "You also go into the vineyard, and I will pay you whatever is right." So they went. When he went*

out again about noon and about three o'clock, he did the same. And about five o'clock he went out and found others standing around; and he said to them, "Why are you standing here idle all day?" They said to him, "Because no one has hired us." He said to them, "You also go into the vineyard."

Scene 2

Now his elder son was in the field; and when he came and approached the house, he heard music and dancing. He called one of the slaves and asked what was going on. He replied, "Your brother has come, and your father has killed the fatted calf, because he has got him back safe and sound."

When evening came, the owner of the vineyard said to his manager, "Call the laborers and give them their pay, beginning with the last and then going to the first." When those hired about five o'clock came, each of them received the usual daily wage. Now when the first came, they thought they would receive more; but each of them also received the usual daily wage.

Scene 3

Then he became angry and refused to go in. His father came out and began to plead with him. But he answered his father, "Listen! For all these years I have been working like a

And when they received it, they grumbled against the landowner, saying, "These last worked only one hour, and you have made them equal to us who have borne the burden of the day

slave for you, and I have never disobeyed your command; yet you have never given me even a young goat so that I might celebrate with my friends. But when this son of yours came back, who has devoured your property with prostitutes, you killed the fatted calf for him!"

and the scorching heat."

Then the father said to him, "Son, you are always with me, and all that is mine is yours. But we had to celebrate and rejoice, because this brother of yours was dead and has come to life; he was lost and has been found."
(Luke 15:11-12, 25-32)

But he replied to one of them, "Friend, I am doing you no wrong; did you not agree with me for the usual daily wage? Take what belongs to you and go; I choose to give to this last the same as I give to you. Am I not allowed to do what I choose with what belongs to me? Or are you envious because I am generous?"
(Matthew 20:1-15[1])

Listeners familiar with these stories' Gospel contexts may have difficulty trusting the full range of their feelings. Because they have learned to assume that the beneficiaries of the superiors' generosity—the late-coming workers and the returning younger son—represent late-coming Christians, such listeners may not readily allow into awareness their sympathies for the hard-working early laborers and the hard-working elder son.

The elder son's anger and the early laborers' resentment are founded on a widely accepted premise: because I have worked harder and more faithfully, I should be given more. The element of comparison is central:

if I work at the same task longer or more effectively than those around me, I deserve more (and "more" is always relative). Almost everyone everywhere embraces this belief. In both of these stories, however, the superior character is unmoved by such comparisons; each insists that the complainers have already received all that is coming to them.

Some listeners, however, find that their uncomfortable feelings persist. Could it be that the elder brother and the early workers have reason to be angry? Many have a hard time trusting this nagging doubt. The complaint of the subordinates seems to challenge the generosity of the superiors. How can one question generosity, particularly when its providers have been faithful to their promises? On behalf of himself and the prodigal's father, the landowner emphatically criticizes such carping. "Is your eye evil because I am good?"

I will take up first that portion of the Prodigal Son I am calling an Elder Son and a Father.

Giving So Much and Receiving So Little

> Now his elder son was in the field;
> and when he came and approached
> the house, he heard. . . .

This segment of the parable begins, once again, with the father structuring its opening scene—this time not by his provision but by his neglect. Throughout lengthy preparations and during the beginning celebration, the father remains unaware of his firstborn. "The sudden appearance of the elder son creates an effect on the listener similar to the father's experience of that son: he has been forgotten. . . . The father, when indulging the son who has slighted him, slights the son who has indulged him."[2]

The father forgets his compliant son because what matters now, and what has always mattered to this generous man, is not what his children supply him but what he supplies them. Limited to providing, the father is confident he has already given his elder son all that he needs. It is about this matter of good-enough provision that son and father begin to quarrel.

> "For all these years I have been
> working like a slave for you . . .

yet you have never even given me. . . ."

*"Son, you are always with me and all
that is mine is yours. . . ."*

It is hard to imagine a wider degree of mutual misperception than the one enclosed by these two quotes. The elder son, certain that he has been deprived of what really matters, perceives himself unable to gain even the slightest hint of his father's responsive recognition. The father, certain of the adequacy of his providing, sees no reason at all why his son should be angry with him. The distance between the two of them is enormous.

In his complaint the elder son names the trouble, but he cannot describe it. "You have never even given me. . . ." The son knows something is lacking but believes it to be his father's recognition; the father counters with an insistence that he has given everything. Both are blocked in their effort to identify what the trouble is by their ready agreement that the father must be the one to give and the son must be the one to take.

Both sons have been endangered by their father's provision. His imposing on them control of his own resources revokes the right of his children to experience the consequences of having to choose. But also foreclosed are those opportunities for growth that regularly follow the achievement of openly expressed opposition. Neither son learns that he can challenge his parent and thrive. Through a "militantly over-protective anticipation,"[3] the father meets every need and erases any conflict. The sons are allowed to want only what their father has to give. Being the only one able to provide, the father's indulgence has rendered his sons dependent, has kept himself in emotional control, and has excluded their protest. Here may be located the essence of the elder son's complaint.

The father's response may be, in its irony, profoundly painful. "All that is mine," says the father, "is yours." For what the father does not possess he cannot give, namely, a life-sustaining insistence that each of his sons find himself through his own work and on his own terms.

Both sons, finally, yield to their father's need and falter toward themselves. Where the younger tried to escape by further destroying distinctions, the elder tries to belong by relying on distinctions that have already been destroyed. Where the younger, defining himself in opposition, was unable to achieve sufficient confidence in his own abilities, the elder, defining himself in compliance, is unable to achieve sufficient confidence in his own worth.

Even if the elder should eventually choose to follow in his father's footsteps, and even if compelled to do so by the economics of that era, that choice properly comes from within the son in his own time. The father's failure to recognize, allow, and protect his son's right to decide prevents the latter from expressing open difference. Such conflict, worked through, might have resulted in emotional separation—a possibility the father, in his turn, may have anticipated as intolerable.

Paternal Failure and Fraternal Envy

In their efforts to fulfill their father's need to be needed, both sons betray their own becoming. The first is rendered falsely guilty ("I have sinned against . . . you") and the second falsely demanding ("You have never . . . given me. . . ."). Because neither has been able to separate from his father, each remains held in rivalry with his brother. Both believe that the inclusion of his sibling means the exclusion of himself. Neither grasps that both are unable to grow as long as their father's needs take precedence over their own.

During the two periods in the story when each son is described as isolated and on his own, one may observe a contrasting sense of time. Where the younger proceeds along a large, single trajectory of flight, profligacy, limit, repentance, and return, the elder is trapped in small, constantly repeating cycles; he enters into his own competencies, complains about his father's unresponsiveness, and remains unable to change either his father or himself. In control of everything, he is in control of nothing.[4]

As is common enough, failure within a previous generation is transformed into envy within the next. How might the elder, in his refusal to engage in risk, envy his brother's maddening flight from consequence? How might the younger, in his fear of responsibility, secretly desire the seemingly effective compliance of the elder? Each discovers, exaggerated within his sibling, a misshapen representation of his own excluded longing.

By focusing one's attention on the distorted responses of the two sons, the parable draws the listener away from wondering how each has been distorted in their relating to each other by their father's overprotection.

Remaining Stuck by Insisting the Other Move

His elder son was in the field. . . .
He . . . approached the house. . . .
He refused to go in. . . .

The elder son does not range far from his father's side. He knows neither the exhilaration of flight nor the risks of return. Certainly he does not contemplate the recklessness of spontaneous expression. Premised on careful obedience, his is the world of control and prediction. He believes merely, simply, that his compliance will result in his maturity. In the parable he barely moves, coming in from the field to the edge of the house. He plants himself squarely within this in-between moment and stands, enraged and still.

He will not move for at least two reasons: first, because he has based his self-confidence on his father's responsiveness and second, because his father will not give it. As a result, he has no way of finding out, were he openly to relinquish compliance, whether he and his father would have the resources to go on. Would he, by becoming a separate, independent adult, matter to his father and matter to himself? The son dares not find out.

The son's anger—which hides this anxiety—is provoked not so much by the father's response to his brother's failure as by his father's failure to respond to himself. The elder's dutifulness is transformed into anger when he suddenly perceives his father's bias. Returning from the field, where he believes he has been working on his father's behalf and with his father's approval, he encounters, hidden within his father's surprising welcome, his father's surprising neglect. He abruptly confronts how his father is more excited by restoring inability than by recognizing ability. Perhaps the greatest hope in this portion of the narrative is the emergence of the elder's anger. Now, at last, he has begun to think for himself.[5]

But he has a long way to go. In his imagination his father continues to dominate all of his resources for self-approval. Unable to achieve an independent self-confidence, the son keeps searching for his father's recognition. He remains stuck by insisting that his father move. For him it is his father's task, as always, to resolve his difficulties.

The son prolongs a futile quest for a father who will provide more than provision, who will develop into other than the mother of an infant, who will express a confident anticipation of his son's own, separate achievements, and who will thereby become truly excited about his son's autonomous functioning. The son does not yet grasp that his father cannot fulfill this longing; instead he persists in attributing his father's unresponsiveness to a lack, not within the father, but within himself.

Unable either to connect or to separate, the two circle each other relentlessly. The son is sure there is still something missing; the father sees nothing missing at all. The child continues to feel in need; the parent insists everything has already been given.

Pulling Back in Order to Go Forward

This part of the parable may provide, through a balancing of possibilities, a masterful ambiguity. I have been developing one side; the other is well-known. Can this father, so widely admired as someone who provides and forgives, also be someone who deprives and controls? Can this son, so readily understood as passive and resentful, also be someone struggling for his emotional survival?

If the listener chooses to pursue these latter possibilities, she or he can perceive in the elder's suffering an effort to compel his father to become a father—in response to his father's effort to keep his son a child.[6] Each, in isolation from the other, might then be revealed as enmeshed in an endless struggle to control the other.

Such a listener following such a choice might then wonder if any resolution exists. How can a child caught up in what is missing in his father discover what is missing in himself? If this son could accept his father's inability, abandon his quest, and look elsewhere for discipline and recognition, would he not be able to get on with his life?[7] But then what might happen to his father?

I believe the tensions in this portion of Two Sons and a Father resonate well with the tensions in the Vineyard Workers (or, as I have titled it, Laborers and a Landowner). To expose this possibility requires an initial exploration of the latter's larger dimensions.

Acting Justly or Just Being Civilized?

The parable I am calling Laborers and a Landowner may well be exploring a pervasive conflict present in first-century Roman-occupied Jewish Palestine.[8] This small, crossroads country had for centuries been mediating between two contending cultural perspectives: (1) the Hellenistic (or Greco-Roman) norm of civilized custom, and (2) the Hebraic norm of divine justice. The Hellenistic norm likely had the allegiance of the landed aristocracy, who for hundreds of years had been steadily expropriating peasant land. (This chronic aristocratic expropriation had forced many land-owning peasants into the marginal under-class of day laborers.[9]) The Hebraic norm, incorporating the concept that the Land belonged to Yahweh, probably remained far more attractive to the vulnerable peasantry.[10]

The English translation of the parable (with its significant phrases in boldface) does not make this tension between the Hellenistic and Hebraic norms readily evident.

> *[The landowner] said to [some day laborers], "You also go into the vineyard, and I will pay you* **whatever is right."**

> *[Some of the day laborers] grumbled against the landowner. . . . But he replied to one of them, "Friend, I am* **doing you no wrong. . . ."**

The landowner tells some of his day-laborers that he will pay them "whatever is right." Translated here is the Greek word *dikaios*, which originally denoted "connection with tradition or custom, and therefore, applied to a person, indicates 'one who conforms, who is civilized, who observes custom.'"[11] Yet, when this same word enters the Hebrew Bible in its third-, second-, and first-century B.C.E. Greek translations (together termed "the Septuagint"), its Greek meanings are subsumed under ancient Hebrew meanings. In the Hebrew Bible "the [Hellenistic] concept of virtue is replaced by the basic question of how man is to stand before the judgment of God expressed in the Law as a standard. If in the rest of the Greek world a man is *dikaios* who satisfies ordinary legal norms, fulfilling his civic duties in the most general sense, here the *dikaios*, is the man who fulfills his duties towards God and the theocratic society, meeting God's claim in this relationship."[12]

Jesus' native language was almost certainly Aramaic; some suppose he was also fluent in Greek.[13] Even if first told in Aramaic, it may still be that this parable moves between these very different Hellenistic and Hebraic understandings of "what is lawful" and "what is just." Twice the parable appears to make a play on these differences.

Hoping to Be Honorable While Given to Greed

Earlier in the day the landowner volunteers to some of the day laborers an ambiguous message: he intends to pay them "whatever is right." Does he mean, in the Hellenistic sense, "what is right according to custom" or does he mean, in the Hebraic sense, "what is just in the eyes of God"?

By the end of the day, however, the landowner has moved away from his earlier ambiguity. By evening, when the work is done, he claims to be limiting himself merely to what is lawful. He says, "Am I not allowed to do what I choose with what belongs to me?" The Greek *ouk exestin moi* means, more literally, "Is it not lawful for me. . . ?" or "Is it not permitted me . . . ?" He is no longer appealing, albeit ambiguously, to what might be understood as God's just ways; he has now limited himself to customary legal obligations. Under cover of generously enhancing the expected daily wage, the landowner may have shifted the terms of his publicly declared honor.

Yet the owner cannot seem to free himself from his ambivalent desire to fit into the Hebraic norm. Using a double negative, he returns a second time to his ambiguous claim to be just. He describes his actions to a complaining day laborer with these words: "I am doing you no wrong." The Greek is *ouk adiko se*. The verb here, *adikeo*, is from the same stem as the earlier *dikaios*. The landowner's phrase literally means, "I am not doing to you what is not right," or, in the Hebrew, biblical sense, "I am doing you no injustice." Strip away the double negative and there remains the echo of his earlier seeming promise to be just.

In this reading, using the perspective of a Hebrew listener, the landowner's generosity obscures the larger obstacles to his ambiguous desire. If he declares, "I will pay you what is just," but then claims, "Am I not allowed to do what I choose with what belongs to me?" he appears caught in a contradiction. Central here may be the conflicted effort of the landowner, possessed both with unchecked power and with the desire to appear just, to pursue self-interest under the guise of apparent rectitude.

Only the owner's definition of what constitutes the customary wage—without any input from the laborers—becomes the basis for any later decision about what might be perceived as generosity. This benchmark turns out to be, of course, whatever the owner's social class long ago determined it would be. Certainly well-known in Mediterranean antiquity was how the landed aristocracies of that period, devoted to the integrity of Roman law, maintained their laborers at subsistence levels.[14]

After researching the probable value of this usual daily wage, Herzog concludes, "because the day laborer worked so infrequently. . . . [a] denarius a day would not [even] sustain life."[15]

The landowner's assertion that he collaborated in setting the wage ("Did you not agree with me for the usual daily wage?") represents either self-deception or else a deliberate insult. Given a market flooded with impoverished, unemployed workers, the owner knows full well that none of these laborers can bargain with him. What is lawful or customary, to which standard the landowner later appeals, is, in the politics of that era, solely the decision of his narrowly based class.[16] Although codified into customary law, this decision is insulated from any criteria of divine justice; it is open to no outside challenge. Indeed, the amount or intensity of the laborers' work—or of any effort on their part to negotiate—has nothing at all to do with what the owner decides he will pay. Yet he chooses to describe himself as someone entering into agreement with persons capable of independent bargaining, not as someone able to dominate a class of laborers wholly vulnerable to his self-interest.[17]

In a world of unequally distributed resources and subsistence daily wages, the landowner in fact cannot realize his ambition to "pay what is just" out of what "belongs" to him until much more of what belongs to his landowning class belongs to the day-laborer class.[18] If one believes that in his desire to be good the landowner is aspiring to justice, then at issue that evening may not be a decision about the worth of twelve hours of labor but rather a judgment about hundreds of years of land-grabbing.

Because the underlying inequalities on which he depends would not permit it, the landowner's generosity cannot produce substantive change. To maintain his position, this aristocrat must continue to pay his laborers less than subsistence wages. Like the slave-owner in an earlier parable, for him truly to succeed in being generous, the entire social structure of which he is a part would have to be transformed.

Voicelessness

The early workers sense that something is wrong, but their complaint is off the mark; they are unable to articulate the trouble. Like the slave in a Slave and a Master, they have awareness sufficient only to accept the superior's definition of what is "lawful" or "customary."[19] Never having experienced a framework of justice, they lack the resources to imagine its contours.

Such work falls to the listener. Modern readers may have a hard time estimating the sufficiency of the customary wage of a denarius a day but they should have no difficulty judging which party in this landowner-laborer twosome actually determined how much that customary wage would be—and how that party might rationalize a less-than-equitable amount.

The early workers' calculation, "one denarius for one hour's work should mean more for twelve hour's work," may in the parable function as a large distraction. What may instead be both central and hidden is how the landowner (all the time making less than subsistence wages his benchmark) chooses to call upon both laborers and listeners alike to recognize him as someone who is generous and even as someone who is just.

If one does not notice his prior position of total control over the essential definitions, the landowner indeed appears to be generous. (Traditional readings rely on this generosity to render him a figure for God.) Yet oppressed peoples the world over are endlessly familiar with the differences between what is held out to them as lawful and what they themselves perceive to be just.[20]

Thus, the anger of the early laborers may be located not only in their response to perceived inequity but also in their inarticulate reaction to the landowner's unacknowledged arrogance.[21] They are acutely sensitive to the way in which this aristocrat unilaterally defines who deserves

what—and especially to how he dares, relying on such prejudiced definitions, to declare himself "good."

A Too-Insistent Voice

Without the landowner's generosity, the early workers would not have
objected; yet his unexpected gifts provoke a complaint that has little to
do with his generosity. That generosity, rather, may serve to distract
owner, laborers, and listeners alike from the true sources of the laborers'
anger.

As with the elder son, the laborers know something is wrong. But the
problem is not what they are complaining about; they simply do not
have the words with which to say it. Neither, in this reading, does the
landowner. Not only are the laborers being presented with deprivation as
if it were generosity, so also the landowner is proffering citizenship as if
it were justice.

A description of his self-deception begins with this aristocrat's need to
portray himself as good. Why is he not content merely to exploit? Why
does he spend so much energy going not once but four times to the
marketplace? Why not send his manager? Why is he so interested in
defending his actions to his day laborers? Again, why not interpose his
manager? If all day long he has been calculating his generosity, is not
such calculation evidence of his self-doubt? The owner goes a long way
out of his way—too far, in my judgment—in order to make his case.

I believe the landowner fails to estimate his labor needs efficiently
because he has another goal in mind. At the start of his day he knows full
well what he hopes to accomplish at its end: he intends to demonstrate
his goodness. This wealthy man goes himself four times to the marketplace not only in search of labor but also in search of honor.

Such a longing may account for the owner's reversal of the customary
order in which laborers are paid. Herzog makes much of this reversal; he
rightly perceives that the owner's intent is to humiliate the early workers.
I would add that his need to shame others (he could have given everyone
a proportionate bonus) is evidence of anxiety about shamefulness in
himself.

Nowhere does the owner openly declare his desire for honor. Instead,
he crafts a drama designed to put blame on his victims and in the process

elevate himself. By demeaning the worth of their only possession, their labor, he deliberately humiliates the early workers. He then counters their predictably angry response with a prepared appeal to his generosity.

The landowner expends considerable energy trying to convince these same laborers that he is a decent person. But he protests too much. "I will pay you what is right." "I have done you no injustice." Finally, using as evidence a generosity funded by parasitism, he arrogantly tells these impoverished workers, "I am good."[22]

The owner, by a careful engineering of his subordinate's response, enables himself to exit from this drama reassured of his own rectitude. He leaves, moreover, convinced that any anger in his laborers represents merely their envy at his sudden generosity—and could not possibly be the result of his chronic stinginess. But I believe the landowner, by the evidence of his insistent efforts, will remain uncertain of his honor. By his immersion in a religious culture traditionally focused on justice, he is in a dilemma. How can he participate in exploiting others and still go about believing himself to be an honorable man?

Using Generosity to Cover Up Control

In my readings of both these parables, the superiors, appearing to create a new order, intervene in such a way as to maintain the old. Seeming to want change, they in fact block it. Both rely on gift-giving to cover up control. Hiding behind their generosity, the superiors continue to impose their definitions. Worse, they tack on an additional, enraging demand; in seeming innocence they insist, "My good actions should make you feel differently than what you are feeling."[23]

The father's generous provision and the owner's generous wages, by disguising their control, make difficult any coherent rejoinder. Both the elder son and the early workers are unable adequately to describe their distress; inequality renders them inarticulate. How can they discover— much less organize—their own perspectives if both father and landowner remain magnanimously in complete control? In the end they are reduced to an ungrateful rejection of their superior's supposed generosity.

Immersion in these narratives can lead to a growing awareness that they enclose unintegrated ways of seeing. The point of view of the landowner is not the same as that of the laborers. What the father believes his elder son feels may not at all be what the son is actually feeling. Lacking reciprocal speech, each parable protagonist has no way to grasp the other's perspective. Only the listener is positioned to perceive the very different experiences of both persons.

But often listeners grasp only one side—that of the superior. This limit occurs in part because onto this blocking of reciprocal speaking is superimposed the appearance of authoritative speech. The parable's third scene offers the returning superior as the authoritative judge of what has happened.

The last scene of Laborers and a Landowner, however, may be describing what often happens between the economically powerful and the economically weak, namely, how poor people are rarely allowed to speak their minds and how rich people escape having to acknowledge their own perfidy. Our identification with the wealthy tempts us not to question the owner's point of view. Listeners who are poor may know better; they may recognize that the rich have the last word not because they have a firmer grasp on reality but simply because that is how it is with wealthy people.[24]

Despite their very different economic conditions, a comparison of the two parables reveals a consistent pattern of impasse. The laborers respond within a context of chronic deprivation; the elder son reacts within a precocious entitlement. But neither can articulate the sources of their rage. Because generosity shuts down their subordinates' ability to tell them what the trouble is, both superiors remain naive about their misperceptions; they continue to believe they have behaved constructively. Their unequal power results in their isolation. They exit convinced of their goodness.

These parables may be proposing that the kingdom of God, or the reign of God, or the intent of God, or the longing of God (however one terms this core element of Jesus' teaching), may be found in that opening up of space between the misunderstandings of two persons—or of two social classes, or of two nations—where some possibility of creative reconciliation might be grasped. The work of the listener may be to imagine how, in spite of these polarizing and infuriating impasses, each based on the seemingly beneficent use of wealth, both parties might find ways to speak more honestly to the other.

8

How Are These Stories Told
—and Heard?

How Are These Stories Told?

Jesus told these parables, I believe, to evoke in the hearer both how things are and how God yearns for them to be. This yearning in God, this longing in God, Jesus called "the kingdom of God." God entrusts to the listener the way things are and waits, with hope, for the listener to discern how they are meant to be. At the center of this powerfully ironic vision, at the heart of the rule of God on earth, God is dependent. God relies on the hearer both to discover what is wrong and to reach for its corrective.

I perceive the seven parables of this book, in their very structure, to embody this vision. More than anything else, I believe it is this embodiment that identifies them as coming from a single creative genius. When engaging the balanced misperceptions that have enveloped the two parable protagonists, the only one separate enough from their entangled histories, the only one able to imagine a different outcome, is the listener. Thus, these parables entrust their outcomes to those outside their boundaries; the listener alone is empowered to determine not only what has happened but what will happen. So positioned, the listener encounters what may be the central question these parables explore: How is it possible, having included some by excluding others, to include everyone?

Another version of this same question might be, How is it possible to prevent the oppressed from becoming oppressors? The most common outcome of being oppressed is just such a turning upon a new and weaker other.[1] Regularly absent in this seemingly ineluctable sequence is an opportunity for those who were formerly oppressed to discover, while in the process of becoming oppressors, their own collusion.

In these seven parables, Jesus' approach to this central human dilemma seems to me to be as follows: Teaching in a context where identity had often been developed through excluding others, Jesus begins
these parables by providing an inclusive but isolated place in which
oppressed and oppressor newly try to trust each other. In such an
enclosed space, without anyone else involved, each then attempts to
complete some part of the other's desire. In so doing, however, each has
in some way to struggle with the mixing up of trust with dominance.

This struggle is heightened because these seven parables intermingle
"badness" and "goodness" within and between their major characters.
Each is implicated in the difficulties of the other; none is pure. A rich
man ignores his competent manager; his loyal subordinate ignores his
lord. A slave-master wants his exploited slaves to exploit others; some,
while remaining slaves, try to become masters, but another dramatizes
the demand's unsolvable conflict. Another slave-master tries to forgive
his slave; the latter, with some integrity, insists on imitating him. A
judge compels a persistent presence he disdains; the widow's consequent loss of choice masks her potential for a similar controlling. A
landlord, inappropriately trusting in law, permits his distant tenant
farmers to intensify a hopeless rebellion—and the result is murder upon
murder. A father graciously imposes his own unfinished work upon his
children; his sons in response either squander in despair or demand out
of deprivation. A landowner generously overpays the same laborers he
regularly deprives; some are angry and some are silent but none are
able to articulate either what the trouble is or how they themselves
might be tempted to follow suit.

In all of these accounts, the superior's giving occurs within the context
of a prior and unacknowledged destructiveness. Such disavowed but still
alive destructiveness provokes in the subordinate a destructive response.
The matter now see-saws between them. Each is troubled by the other—
and only the listener is positioned to intervene.

Hidden behind the exit provided by the superior's seemingly final
judgment, Jesus offers his listeners a chance to enter the story by a different route. They may do so by actively supposing how those who may
be oppressors might somehow include the oppressed, and how those
who may be oppressed might somehow include the oppressor.

Such an unobtrusive luring of the listener to participate in the work of completing the story is, in my judgment, a major mark of the authentic parables of Jesus. This shared work is created by the parables' ongoing, unresolved, and exquisitely balanced misperceptions. No one is simply at fault; no one is simply right. Each is involved in the difficulty of the other; all are enmeshed in the troubles of their times, and no one can be included without including the other.

The Presence of Irony

One way these parables may function has recently been the object of much scrutiny: they reverse and overturn what is normally expected. For example, Crossan sees them as integral to all of Jesus' behavior; Jesus' actions in their entirety constitute an attack upon established patterns of expectation.[2] His parables shift and turn inside out what we think we know and confidently expect. For Crossan, parable contrasts with myth. Myth proposes contradictions existing in active tension and moves to resolve those contradictions. Parable, by contrast, introduces conflict where before none is perceived to exist.

I have come to suspect, however, that Crossan's emphasis upon a single, masterful overturning of expectation, initiated within each story by the superior's surprising actions, is more likely the tip of an ironic iceberg.[3] Close examination of each narrative suggests that the superior's action has more the appearance than the substance of change. Far from overturning established ways of perceiving, the superior's gracious or unexpected initiatives may be driving further into concealment the as-yet-unchanged realities of the superior's ongoing control. His blaming—or forgiving—may be full of irony. The stronger may be reduced to challenging the weaker to overcome what he himself has been unable even to see. I believe this irony—and the listener's invitation to experience it—is central to the functioning of these stories.

The presence of such irony is not widely appreciated. Its origins may be discovered in the superior's attempt to include while still excluding. Heard this way, the parables become descriptions of the losses inherent in the superior's attempt to possess—particularly the loss of the excluded other upon whom the one excluding seeks to rely. The superior, by continuing to control, renders his subordinate unable to provide the very responsiveness he seeks.

This irony operates on at least two levels: (1) at the level of the superior's still excluding when trying to include and (2) at the level of the listener's accepting without challenge the distortions required to sustain such inequality.

In these parables the superior appears to himself, to his subordinates, and to listeners alike as one long accustomed to having his way, whether by generosity coupled with coercion (the slave-masters), by generosity coupled with denial (the rich man, the father, and the landowner), or by denial coupled with persistence (the judge and the landlord). This time, however, each superior sets himself the task of engaging a subordinate whom he has chosen to trust. This time he wants not cowed compliance but a willing response. This time he has dared to desire the desire of another.

None of these stories questions the ability of the dominant figure to control. But when that superior becomes ambitious to engage his subordinate in collaboration, when he chooses to try to evoke trust across inequality, he proceeds away from the effectiveness of raw power and toward an altogether different kind of authority. He must now encourage newly awakened freedoms. He has agreed, knowingly or not, to depend on his suddenly empowered subordinate. The latter, abruptly stirred from oppression, must supply of his or her own free will something essential to the task. The known potency of control is now to be translated into the novel conditions of collaboration.

When stretched across new requirements of equality, the common methods of coercion—so familiar as to escape observation—become worse than inadequate. Overtly seeking a risk-taking enabled by collaboration, covertly the superior facilitates a resistance provoked by control. Unable to anticipate other than dominance, the subordinate stumbles when trying to grasp an entrusting so ambiguously extended. These ironies are pervasive. Here is the confrontation of nascent trust with the muted realities of social malaise.

Thus a rich man, full of neglect toward a competent subordinate, cashiers him for neglect. An exploiting slave-master is incensed that one of his exploited slaves does not follow his example. Another slave-master imprisons his slave because the latter imitates him. A seemingly self-sufficient judge demeans the intrusions of a dependency he secretly desires. Because he so much wants to believe himself within the law, a landlord exposes his son to lethal lawlessness. A father fails to suspect that his undisciplined generosity may be destroying his children's ability to discipline themselves. And a landowner sincerely believes his momentary generosity overcomes his chronic depriving.

Some types of irony in these stories may be easier to appreciate than others. Perhaps most available is the irony of trying to include while still excluding, for example, the slave-master who wishes to evoke loyalty to himself while systematically frustrating his slave's loyalty to his own becoming (a pattern not infrequent in parent-child relationships).

More difficult to suppose may be the irony of inclusion hidden within exclusion, for example, the judge's needing, without being aware of it, a responsiveness he both compels and rejects. Most difficult to suspect, probably, is the irony of exclusion hidden within inclusion, for example, the father who, when providing handsomely for his sons, defeats them.

The Nature of the Kingdom of God

How the listener approaches these parables has important implications for two contemporary areas of lively debate about Jesus: (1) Did the historical Jesus self-consciously present himself as the Messiah, or as the apocalyptic Son of Man, or as the Son of God?[4] and (2) What constitutes the range of possible meanings in Jesus' central and paradoxical concept, "the kingdom of God"? I would like here to take up only the second of these two questions.

Biblical scholars devoted to distinguishing an inferred historical Jesus from his later portrayals in the Gospels have throughout this century argued about whether, and in what sequence of historical events, Jesus' teaching concerning the kingdom of God moved (or was moved) from (1) here and now observations concerning divine presence in here and now realities (curiously termed "realized eschatology" and sometimes "sapiental eschatology") to (2) anticipations of the inbreaking of divine power into the course of human history (termed "imminent eschatology") to (3) an expectation of a final Day of Judgment at the end of time, where right will finally and decisively overturn wrong (termed "apocalypticism")—or whether the sequence was in a different or opposite direction. To complicate things, since mid-century major shifts have evolved in the scholarly consensus on these matters.[5]

As I read this debate side by side with my understanding of these parables, I become puzzled by any effort to use them to support categories (2) and (3) above. To me these narratives have nothing to do with the rushing in of an external corrective and everything to do with the chronic misunderstandings of everyday life.

Nonetheless, it has long been debated whether the parables provide clear reference in their internal workings to the idea of apocalyptic, that is, the expectation that at the end time outside forces of right will enter reality and coerce a final rectitude. Indeed, the parables of this book seem constructed so as to lead in that direction; listeners are drawn to agree with the superior character's final judgment; the master or father has finally set things right.

I myself find it difficult to imagine an objective statement of content and a subjective experience of listening more adverse and alien to the idea of an intrusion of justice from some external source than the parable form as understood in this book. Put negatively, I find little in these stories that supports such a stark division into "good" and "bad" essential to end-of-time, Day of Judgment expectations. As apocalyptic is a splitting off of good from bad, so these parables would have to be seen as resolving differences by the elevation of one person at the expense of another.[6] Put positively, the influence of God's power to transform seems to me located not so much in the story's telling of a truth as in its luring of the listener to imagine some means to achieve an eventual reconciliation of its pervasive misunderstandings.

In my understanding the kingdom of God (or the reign or rule or intention of God) is not a static territory.[7] Nor is it simply a future event—at least not as represented in these stories. Because of the carefully developed balance of misunderstandings present between the parable characters, any images within them that suggest divine power breaking into the course of history should be, I believe, subsumed under quite different images, namely, of divine presence luring creative responses from listeners caught up in the specific misperceptions of personal, local, national, and global differences.[8] Put another way, apocalyptic evokes the dream of a catastrophic, definitive transformation of all history, settling and satisfying everything in a single moment. By contrast, I think these stories invite the listener to imagine partial and repeated healings of mundane histories—and to leave much of the work incomplete. As someone commented recently, "We need to have sweeping visions—and the capacity to celebrate small victories."

Widely recognized in Jesus' central metaphor of the kingdom is the paradox of "it is here" combined with "it is coming." I propose that a consonance exists between the nature of the kingdom of God and the structure of these parables: both at the same time are "now-manifest" and "yet-to-come." The narratives, of course, are here present. However, in the sense that they entrust their outcomes to the open-ended uncertainties of listener decision-making, they are yet to come.

The issue here may in part be one of agency: does the agent come from without or arise from within? Apocalyptic anticipates the rushing in of an outside force; its focus is on an externally imposed resolution. By contrast, these parables seem to me to offer the possibility of change only when the listener actively works to create their outcome.

Some of the parables studied here can even be read as satire upon apocalyptic, particularly a Slave and a Master and Two Sons and a Father. In both stories the main character's fortunes are suddenly and completely transformed. Each receives what he believes to be his fondest wish. Each then proceeds to destroy all of the remaining possibilities for positive change. I think a major source of this disaster is that the impetus for change has come upon him not from within but from without; thus co-opted, his response becomes a retaliatory, needful collapse.

"Give me my inheritance now before I have to confront the anxiety of mastering my own life on my own terms." This sentence with irony may capture the desire of many of us in relation to these narratives, namely, to have answers provided from without, from outside our own struggle and our own risk.

How Are These Stories Heard?

Listeners of every generation, each in turn, are invited to engage the enigmas of these stories. This book raises questions, drawn from the perspective of contemporary psychotherapy, about their apparent metaphors of power. In an ongoing psychotherapy, the desire of the client is often, and for a long time, to have the therapist be the agent of change. However, psychotherapists assume that power exercised unilaterally by the therapist and therefore divorced from the willing participation of the client merely results in the latter's compliance and a subsequent loss of creative possibility.

I propose that the massive power of these narratives lies in their reliance upon the listener. In them the empire of God comes upon us, not as an overwhelming corrective but rather as that lure which evokes in us the work of recognizing the very different experience of the other.

These parables seem to me to function as does a therapist, in that they are at the same time both nonpressuring and evocative. As does a therapist, they do not confront the listener with inexorable meaning, nor do they supply clear certainties to support one person's perspective over another. Rather than offering some single understanding able to be translated into prose, they may instead, as does a therapist, receive points of view, hold them, and then hold them up for the listener to observe.

One might perceive the parable form to be addressing us, using the words of Margaret Atwood from quite another context, as follows:

> She will have her own version. I am not the center of her story, because she herself is that. But I could give her something you can never have, except from another person: what you look like from the outside. A reflection. This is the part of herself I could give back to her. We are like the twins of old fables, each of whom has been given half a key.[9]

I believe neither therapist nor parable alone can effect change. Both require the effortful participation of client and listener; meanings and consequent possibilities rely on their contribution. What the parable can do with the listener depends intimately on what the listener realizes she or he is doing with the parable.

What, indeed, is the listener's subjective experience of the parable? Does it press toward us, offering an example or an expectation to be accepted or adopted? Or does it lure us, beckoning with puzzling questions rather than ready answers? Do we perceive imaginative worlds that cohere only by excluding large portions of the other's experience? Or do we struggle to bring together widely contrasting points of view?

I believe there is a parallel between (1) how tragedy unfolds in the parable, because neither participant can recognize the disguised desire of the other, and (2) how the parable relies on the listener to push beyond the superior's final judgment to take measure of those formidable inequalities that lie buried well before its beginning.

Upon entering these narratives you discover yourself involved in inter-dependencies merged tightly together with inequalities. As you work to free yourself and move from one side to the other, you realize you are stretched across wide social and economic differences. You may then assume that such differences are settled fact and have no bearing on what happens. Or you may perceive such histories to be central. You may conclude that the actions of one character have little effect on the actions of the other. Or you may suppose that the two characters are entwined as a unit, so that each, in spite of their differences, shapes and is shaped by the other.

After a time you may realize that you have chosen to locate yourself somewhere among these different possibilities. In particular, either you have identified with one of the two major characters or else you have tried to stay somewhere in between. You realize you have not been able not to choose.

One popular solution to the dilemmas posed by these stories is to join the superior and exclude—through inappropriate blame or forgiveness—the subordinate. However, because they have entered late into a long-developing sequence of misunderstandings, such listeners may fail to recognize (1) the dominant character's ongoing as well as historic oppression, (2) the subordinate's mimicking of that control, and (3) the consequent inability of both to give voice to their very different experiences.

When engaging these stories we are liable to become caught up in the same misperceptions that disable the parable characters; we may discover ourselves colluding in their disabilities. Just as therapists sometimes are not able to extricate themselves from participating in a client's misperceptions, so listeners find themselves doing to the parable characters what the characters themselves have been doing to each other.

We too can neglect the manager's loneliness and dismiss the rich man's isolation. We too can resist empathizing with the dilemma of persons caught between the options of misusing power and falling prey to powerlessness. We too can agree to throw the weaker miscreant into prison while at the same time overestimating the dominant other's capacity to evoke an attitude of compassion. Along with the vineyard owners, we also are capable of using law to rationalize our own probity and exploit others. With landowner and father, we too know how to use generosity to control—just as we know how to ignore the dangerous impact of our giving upon those newly struggling to establish independence.

Both to our chagrin and our opportunity, we can catch ourselves becoming oppressors. Developing an awareness of such collusion can become the seedbed of a larger empathy. Such empathy, in turn, can be the initiator of change. In the process of allowing us to become the ones who exclude, these parables also offer us the chance to readdress the one whom we have made an "it"—the subordinate and perhaps even the superior—as a "thou."

Inclusion Leading to Novel Possibility

When trying to imagine what listener responses might evoke change, three stand out as critical: (1) the need for an observant third to stand in between the two who are estranged; (2) the need to see the entire sequence of events, and (3) the need to imagine how both participants might give voice to their different experiences.[10] No understanding you provide is likely to be complete; instead you try to imagine ways in which both sides might speak to each other—how they might articulate their misperceptions. In this approach, change would come about because each, through the imaginative intervention of you as listener, would empower the other to speak.

What up to this moment had appeared as an ending—because you took sides—now becomes a new position of listening that leads to greater complexity. Things now have a chance to become more than they seem. For example, as the father's forgiveness begins to appear as a further entrapment, the listener begins to wonder, "How might this compassionate father give without undermining his son?"

You as listener can then provide in imagination a gradually developing give and take between the parable participants. Thus, in the story of a Younger Son and a Father, the son might be imagined to say, "Father, I said I wanted you to give me my inheritance but I may not in fact have wanted you actually to agree. I'm not sure what I want from you." Such an openly expressed ambivalence might then draw the father to wonder, "What am I attempting to accomplish by being so willing to give?" He might then address this all-important question to his son, who in turn might feel able to risk describing how ambivalently he has felt about having to test his own competencies. And the father might then find words to express his own profound feelings of loss at the prospect of such success.

Trying to complete these stories through introducing such imaginative inclusions will invariably lead to new beginnings; in whatever way you put these stories together, you have a chance to come upon both your own incompleteness and further possibility. As you ponder the question, "What changes would enable these two persons to hear each other differently?" you realize another, namely, "What changes would enable me to become a better listener?" Wanting the other to change, you realize you also may want to change.

You may then begin to suspect the wider potencies of this peculiar metaphor of power—of estranged persons (including ourselves) dependent on a third to realize change. For these parables may touch upon differences not only between persons, but between groups, tribes, nations, and the largest divisions within the planet itself. Your hope may become not to erase difference, which may be the essence of the perverse,[11] but rather to elaborate difference. You realize you may not be able to include while at the same time excluding others.[12] The final reaches for any listener might be characterized as "a thickening of possibilities."[13]

In my judgment, the parable form with imposing irony represents God's empire as approaching the listener as a vulnerable child.[14] Each listener is free to take the story in a wide array of directions. The narrative neither overwhelms nor resists; rather it waits and evokes, open and accepting. No part of it is so commanding as to compel a specific response. But once the listener chooses to attend, the parable requires choice. To attend is to decide among options. I perceive these parables as offering the listener a chance to do much of the work. In so doing, I see their author as doing the larger portion of the work. As any parent or teacher—or psychotherapist—knows, rather than provide one, it is far more difficult to wait expectantly for a developing answer.

In their very construction, these parables may in fact illustrate Jesus' paradoxical conception of God's now-present and yet-to-come kingdom, or imperial rule, or intention. In them what might be perceived as the dramatic rushing in of divine power may be reconfigured as an evocative, luring presence wholly dependent on listener response. Here then, within the parable form, may be a major paradox: the advent of God's reign

is discovered not in definitive answers but rather in a profound
for the recipient's right, need, and opportunity to respond.

> *The kingdom of God is not coming with things that can be*
> *observed; nor will they say, "Look, here it is!" or "There it is!" For,*
> *in fact, the kingdom of God is among you. (Luke 17:20b-21)*[15]

Appendix

Two Sons and a Father
and the Book of Genesis

A neglected resource for the study of Two Sons and a Father is the book of Genesis.[1] No commentator I know of goes beyond the brief allusions to this possibility.[2]

Much of the book of Genesis is organized around the theme of two sons and a father: Adam (or God) with Cain and Abel; Abraham (or God) with Ishmael and Isaac; Isaac with Esau (or Edom) and Jacob (or Israel); and Jacob with Joseph and his brothers, especially Judah. By way of contrast, the parable omits what Genesis accentuates, namely, the influence of powerful matriarchs: Eve, Sarah, Rebekah, and Rachel.

This largest theme in Genesis discovers a parent standing atop a triangle and choosing the younger of two sons over the elder. Matriarchs and patriarchs, enacting God's desire while contravening God's law (Deut 21:15-17), consistently give the inheritance, birthright, or paternal blessing to the younger son.

The inheritance in question signifies, among other things, the Land. These narratives, presumably composed and fitted together by authors and editors long after the events they purport to describe,[3] seem retroactively to sanction ancient Israel's dominance of Canaan.[4] God chooses the younger son (read: Israel) to receive the inheritance (read: the Land), and God denies the inheritance to the elder son (read: the competing tribes also living in Canaan).

The early hearers of Two Sons and a Father knew these Genesis stories well; both their similarities and their differences with the parable would be noticed and pondered. When, at the outset, the father elects to divide his property, such listeners would discern an allusion to the Genesis accounts of God assigning territory.

The Elder Son

In the parable, hard upon the younger son's return, the elder son is introduced as separated from his father and acting on his own—"in the field." In the Cain story (4:8), the Esau story (25:27), the Joseph story (37:15), and in the parable, "the field" is that place of autonomous functioning, reserved for elder sons, that is both out of sight of the father but within the scope of his assumed desire. As does the youthful Esau, the parable's elder son believes that by placing himself there he is following his father's wishes. It is while he is in "the field" (27:3), however, that Esau is betrayed.

When the elder son of the parable complains bitterly to his father, the Hebrew listener cannot help but hear an echo of the elder Esau's despairing cry, "Bless me, me also, father!" (27:34). The Hebrew listener will also hear in the elder son's complaint, "you have never given me even a young goat . . . ," allusions to the younger Jacob's receiving exactly that paternal resource when complying with the unlawful desires of both matriarch and deity (see 27:9).

The Younger Son

The most renowned of the younger sons of Genesis are Jacob and Joseph. Jacob as a young man has not yet separated from his parents. He exercises little of his own initiative; what he is unable to earn, he instead, with the collusion of both parents[5] proceeds to take. The younger son's imperious "Give me!" must surely for the Hebrew listener resonate with Jacob's importunate "Sell me!" Who is this son who succeeds by demanding what, on his own, he is unable to produce? And who is this parent who intrudes alien resources into a growing adult who needs, above all, some way to discover his own?

Incompetence, Jacob discovers, means gain; competence, Esau learns, means loss. The Hebrew listener to the parable has already imbibed, and now ponders, these themes.

Isolated in a far country while fleeing his brother's vengeance, Jacob utters a bargaining prayer that is echoed in the exhausted younger son's calculating soliloquy ("How many of my father's hired hands have bread enough and to spare. . . ."). "If God . . . will give me bread to eat . . . so that I come again to my father's house in peace, then the LORD shall be my God" (28:20-21).

It is more difficult to suppose those resonances with the parable's younger son that arise from the heroic figure of Joseph. For these correspondences, unlike those derived from Jacob, are the product of contrasts. The trajectory of Joseph is a mirror opposite to that of the parable's younger son.

In the Joseph story, this younger son, in a foreign country, moves from enslavement to a position of great wealth; in the parable, the younger son, in a foreign country, moves from wealth to virtual enslavement. Joseph's rise to power is marked by intense probity and good judgment; the younger son seems motivated by an equally focused effort to fail. Where Joseph, anticipating the worldwide famine to come, stores the produce of all Egypt in vast warehouses, the younger son, lacking even the capacity to anticipate his own hunger, flings his patrimony to the winds. As Joseph seems destined to power, the younger son seems determined to impotence.

In the center of his story, the younger son—contracted to serve a Gentile—is found defeated, resourceless, and unable to feed even himself. In the center of his story, Joseph—also contracted to serve a Gentile—is discovered as supremely confident, superbly competent, and engaged in feeding the entire world.

The final reuniting of father and younger son possesses further parallels, again in reversal. In Genesis, it is the younger son, vicegerent of all Egypt, who rushes to meet his father, falls on his neck and weeps (46:29). In the parable, it is the father who runs to meet his impoverished son, puts his arms around him and kisses him. (And when Esau, the aggrieved elder, finally reunites with his betraying younger brother, it was Esau who runs to meet Jacob, embraces him, and kisses him [33:4].)

The Linking Symbol of "Robe"

The younger son and Joseph share one event in common: both are recipients of a robe proclaiming parental preference. This symbol is a major link between the parable and these patriarchal narratives. In Genesis, "robe" functions as the marker for the (betraying) bestowal of the inheritance by the father upon the younger son.

Jacob deceives his father and steals the inheritance by wearing his elder brother's robe. Having spent much of his life in flight from Esau's anticipated vengeance, Jacob, with amazing obtuseness, arouses a similar murderous jealousy in his own elder sons by cloaking his younger son in a robe of special favor. This same robe will return, torn and bloodied, to deceive the once deceiving father into believing that his beloved Joseph is dead. In the subsequent account of Potiphar's wife, a torn robe reappears as the symbol of betrayal in the midst of being chosen.[6] This symbol's dual function reaches its climax when the august father Pharaoh, raising the younger son Joseph from ignominy to power, clothes him in robes of royal favor.

To choose the younger is to exclude the elder. Here, perhaps, is the fundamental dilemma contained within these Genesis stories: How can the God of all include some and exclude others? The final response in Genesis to this dilemma is stunning. As the story of Joseph progresses, the theme of being chosen is transformed. No longer is exclusion simply the fate of the symbolic progenitors of Israel's later tribal enemies (see 1 Chronicles 18:12-13); instead it becomes the fate of Israel itself.

This last exclusion is the consequence of the earlier, magnificent inclusion. The "robe" (and its companion "ring"), which in the parable are the seemingly unambiguous evidences of the father's favor, derive directly from the parallel symbols of Pharaoh's signet ring and robes of fine linen. These latter symbols, however, far from marking entrance into a stable belonging, instead anticipate the beginnings of a prolonged humiliation.

The dramatic ending of the Joseph saga—and there is no better story in all literature—involving reconciliation and the triumphal entry of Israel into Egypt, is finally rendered the distant adumbration of disaster. What appeared as a transfer of power from Pharaoh to Joseph is revealed as finite and failed. The bestowal of the father's robe and ring upon the privileged younger brother leads, as Genesis closes and the book of Exodus opens, to the precursor of a later exile: Israel's descent into centuries of Egyptian slavery—where no one gave them anything.

Thus "robe," which in Genesis is among the major metaphors to signify God's bestowal upon his chosen people of the Land, also becomes a shifting emblem, first of deception and then of desertion.

How the God of Some Becomes the God of All

What happens when one person or group or nation appears to be favored over another? What are the effects upon the one who is assigned prerogatives and upon the one who experiences their loss? What are the authors and editors of the Torah about? What in turn might Jesus be doing by lifting his narrative so deftly from within the strands of this anciently revered consensus?

Crossan[7] refers to Levi-Strauss's "basic thesis that myth performs the specific task of mediating irreducible opposites." In another context Crossan[8] observes, "aniconic monotheism [that is, a monotheism not shaped in human or animal form, not reducible to particulars] is Israel's challenge to itself and the world."

Using these two ideas, it may be that the Genesis narratives, among other things, mediate the following two irreducible opposites: (1) a monotheism not shaped in human or animal form, i.e., not reducible to particulars, and (2) Israel's possession of the particular Land—with the consequent exclusion of others.

Jesus' parables may be understood as his response to those particularist tendencies of any time and place that include some and exclude others. (The challenge here attributed to Jesus in relation to exclusionary tendencies within some forms of the Judaism of his time applies, of course, with equal force to those exclusionary practices endemic to much of later Christianity.)

The metaphor of "the Land"—possession and control over a space that excludes others—readily translates into contemporary ideas of control over a center of meaning, a reality existing "out there," which "could be discerned independently of our perception and our understanding of it."[9] In this light the younger son's demand, "Give me the portion [of the inheritance] that falls to me" may represent a desire for certainty, and the father's giving the deceptive gift of seeming certainty.

But what in Two Sons and a Father can be possessed if the parable has no center, no locus of authority, if the father fails his sons to a degree equivalent to the loss of integrity in each of his sons? The parable presents a total resolution or a total impasse or a potentially restorative balancing, depending on listener perception. Following the third option, one may say that the parable's response to the Genesis problem of inclusion and exclusion involves a double-take. In the Genesis narratives it looks as if someone is being included at the cost of someone being excluded. In the parable, it also looks as if someone has been included and another excluded.

For Jacob to possess the blessing, Esau must be betrayed. For Israel to possess the Land, Edom must be conquered. For Joseph to become a prince, Israel must be enslaved. For a father to provide the inheritance, his sons must fail to grow.

One possible question raised by these sequences may involve how the God of some becomes the God of all. One possible answer may be that God participates equally with all, yearns equally across their various struggles, and holds with equal profundity the limited hopes of each.

Close examination of the parable reveals that, in fact, no one has been chosen or dismissed. Each character remains caught in the other's distress. Each, as a consequence, may hold some form of resolution for the impasse of the other. Yet each must discover larger areas of his own responsibility.

The father may need his elder son's anger to grasp the significance of his younger son's absence, displayed both in the latter's earlier flight and subsequent wordlessness. The younger son, in turn, may need his brother's eventual awareness that the father is unable to provide recognition for both the absent and present competencies of either child. And to reach this point the elder may need the younger's capacity to flee what, in his father, cannot be changed by even the most loyal compliance. All three are entwined in a complex web of misunderstandings that none can disentangle by himself.

The response of Two Sons and a Father to the Genesis problem of choosing some and excluding others may be to present an exquisitely balanced, constantly supple equidistance between the positions of father, younger son, and elder son—between the attitudes of superior and subordinate, haves and have-nots, nation and nation, religious persuasion and religious persuasion, in-group and out-group, the included and the excluded.

Acknowledgments

I extend my grateful appreciation

- to my early teachers in biblical studies: my father, L. Stanley Ford; John Crocker; and Robert A. Moss

- to my later teachers, who first showed me the rich resonances between the biblical tradition and psychodynamic psychotherapy: Lars I. Granberg and James N. Lapsley, Jr.

- to my teachers in psychodynamic psychotherapy: Martin Cooperman, Anne F. deGersdorff, Erik H. Erikson, Elizabeth S. Oakes, William J. Richardson, Eduardo R. Val, Ess A. White, Jr., and Otto A. Will, Jr.

- to James Earl Breech, whose book, *The Silence of Jesus,* and especially its twelfth chapter, became an important impetus to the creation of this book

- to John Dominic Crossan, whose books across three decades have consistently expanded and enlivened my understanding

- to my students at Williams College, especially Michelle M. Freemer, David A. Garfield, and Elizabeth H. Listerman

- to the readers and welcome critics of various drafts of this manuscript: Susan Bingham, Linda E. Comstock, Susan A. deGersdorff, Jean Donati, Esther A. Haskell, David C. Kearns-Preston, Janet Keep, Anne R. Kirchmier, Arthur V. Lee, Jean Lee, Donella Markham, Richard E. Markham, John T. O'Connor, Rob Riggan, Arnold I. Thomas, and especially Karen L. Ford, John S. Ford, Todd A. Sumner, and Eric Youngquist

- to my editor at Fortress Press, J. Michael West, for his clarity, balance, and hard work

- to my clients, who have taught me again and again to listen

- to best friends and steadfast encouragers throughout this long process: Allen M. Comstock and Carol Pepper

- and to my wife, Jina, whose warmth, presence, and confidence have been essential.

Notes

Introduction

1. Sixty versions of thirty-three parables attributed to Jesus of Nazareth survive. Thirty-nine of these versions are found in the three canonical Gospels of Mark, Matthew, and Luke. (Mark has five, Matthew fourteen, and Luke twenty.) Fifteen are in the Gospel of Thomas, originally written in Greek and surviving in a Coptic manuscript discovered in Egypt in 1945. The six remaining versions, none considered authentic to Jesus, are located in the Apocryphon of James, 1 Clement, the Didache, and the Gospel of the Nasoreans. (These facts and opinions are summarized from Funk, Scott, and Butts, eds.: 26-27, 32-33, 40-41, 49-51, 54-55. and 98-99.)

The parable form as developed by Jesus is often introduced by descriptions that distinguish it from parables in the Hebrew Bible and from later rabbinic parables. See, for example, Westermann; Thoma and Wyshogrod, eds., and Stern. For an excellent introduction to the parables of antiquity, see Scott: 3-62.

2. Whether each of these seven parables may reasonably be attributed to the historical Jesus remains the subject of some debate. One comprehensive evaluation of all the parables ascribed to Jesus, made by between forty-two and fifty North American New Testament scholars (Funk, Scott, and Butts., eds.), generally agrees that the historical Jesus is the author of the structure or outline (but not the exact words) of these seven narratives. I believe this position is accepted by the majority of contemporary scholars.

For my own rationale supporting this understanding, see chap. 8. For an alternate point of view, one that attributes authorship of these same parables to the various editors of the Gospels in which they appear, see Drury, 1985: 64-65, 92-93, 104-05, 141-42, 149, 152-53.

3. The theme of the Unjust Judge is a mirror opposite of the other six parables here studied. Instead of entrusting something of value, the superior character (the judge) withholds it; instead of receiving something of value, the subordinate character (the widow) is deprived. See chaps. 4 and 5.

4. There is a strong gender bias in these stories. Of their fifteen major characters, only one is female. What should become clear, however, is how profoundly these narratives describe, expose, and question any relationship based on inequality.

5. For the boundaries of what constitutes the parable proper and what is the

contribution of later Gospel editors, I follow that portion of scholarly consensus represented in Funk, Scott, and Butts, eds.

6. Psychotherapists, of course, have no corner on these ways of listening. What playwrights, novelists, and careful observers have always known, psychotherapists have attended to, systematized, and taught. My perspective and those of my psychotherapy teachers are grounded in the work of Sigmund Freud. For an excellent introduction to the contemporary conduct of psychotherapy from this point of view, see the three volumes by Basch.

7. Here are three examples of how a psychotherapist, when listening to parables, might wonder about what is missing: (1) For he Dishonest Steward: a seemingly insignificant use of words ("my master is taking [not: has taken] the position away from me. . . .") suggests a significant gap in the rich man's behavior. (2) For the Wicked Tenants: the behavior of neither party makes apparent sense. The landowner imagines the murderous tenants are law-abiding; the tenant farmers imagine they can get away with murder. (3) For the Prodigal Son: What feelings are evoked in an observer when a competent adult divests himself of control over his assets in favor of a manifestly immature son?

8. See, for example, the useful summary of the Synoptic Gospel editors' varying perspectives on the parables found in Drury (1987:427-34).

9. One ground-breaking exception to the propensity among modern commentators, until very recently (see the work of Fortna, Herzog, Kahler, Kaylor, Ngugi, and Rohrbaugh), to see the dominant parable character as largely "good" and the subordinate as largely "bad" is found sporadically in the work of James Breech (1983). Breech at times approaches the then-novel proposition that "good" and "bad" are intermingled within and between the unequal parable protagonists. (An earlier but less convincing description of such intermingling is found in Derrett's [1960-61] commentary on The Dishonest Steward. See chap. 1, n. 5).

Given the revolutionary quality at that time of his insight, it is not surprising that Breech applies it unevenly. On the one hand, in his treatment of the Dishonest Steward, Breech (101-13) remains squarely within the usual readings, if anything overemphasizing the traditional tendency to split the two main characters into "good" and "bad." On the other hand, when approaching the Prodigal Son, Breech (184-212) enters new territory. He begins to demonstrate how the attitudes and behaviors of one character infiltrate and provoke the responses of the other, as well as how the economic and generational inequalities of the two father-son pairs are intermingled with their balanced interdependencies. I am indebted to Breech for stimulating my own attempts to understand how each character's actions are shaped by his perceptions of the other's perceptions of him.

10. This holding by the same narrative of differing interpretive possibilities is consonant with Alter's (18,12) view of narration in the Hebrew Bible: "An elaborate system of gaps between what is told and what must be inferred has been artfully contrived to leave us with at least two conflicting, mutually complicating interpretations of the motives and states of knowledge of the principal charac-

ters. An essential aim of the innovative technique of fiction worked out by the ancient Hebrew writers was to produce a certain indeterminacy of meaning, especially in regard to motive, moral character, and psychology. . . . Meaning, perhaps for the first time in narrative literature, was conceived as a process requiring continual revision—both in the ordinary sense and in the etymological sense of seeing-again—continual suspension of judgment, weighing of multiple possibilities, brooding over gaps in the information provided.

11. A group of interpreters, a kind of "school of thought," has particularly emphasized variability in listener understanding of these narratives. Their general approach, led by scholars such as John Dominic Crossan, Robert W. Funk, and Dan O. Via Jr. (see especially Funk, ed., 1974), was prosecuted intensively in North America during the 1970s. These authors began, as do I, by removing the parables from their later Gospel contexts. They then adapted strategies developed by French structuralism, based on ideas drawn particularly from the work of Claude Levi-Strauss.

These researchers chose not to concentrate on the protagonists' perspectives and motives; they instead focused on the fundamental structures of the stories themselves. They sought to demonstrate how the listener's experience is orchestrated by these underlying structures. For example, they understood the parables to provoke in the listener a reversal of expectation.

The work of Crossan and others decisively broke apart the century-old insistence, begun by Adolf Julicher (1888-89), that these narratives should be reduced to "single points." An important development within this general approach was the then novel emphasis on potential variability in listener response. Yet what supported their expectation of "polyvalence," or multiplicity of meaning, was not the range of listener contribution (which is what I stress) but rather the peculiarly unsettling aspects of the parables' construction.

12. See Scott 264, 265; Crossan (1973) 26, 27, 76.

Chapter 1

1. Unless otherwise indicated, all biblical translations are are from *The Holy Bible, New Revised Standard Version*.

A debate exists in the literature as to whether verse 8a is part of this parable. Verse 8a reads, literally, "And commended the master the manager of unrighteousness because shrewdly he acted." Scholars disagree whether the "master" (Greek: *kyrios*) here refers to the rich man of the parable or to Jesus, who purportedly is speaking in the verses immediately following.

I follow those who place 8a within the parable, for example, Fitzmeyer (27-28), Fuchs (4-5), Funk, Scott, and Butts, eds. (32), Scott (260), Topel (218), and Via (156), the major reason being that without this sentence the parable, unlike all the others in this book, has no concluding third scene. For examples of those who exclude 8a from the parable, see Crossan (1974c:206; see also 1973:109; 1991:xxv) and Breech (102). Scott (256-60) provides a review of the debate.

2. Breech 107, 108.

3. Herzog (233-58) makes an intriguing choice at this early point. He avoids the difficulties I am about to face by provoking different ones. He proposes (233) that the charge of squandering against the manager is false; it represents hostile rumors manufactured by the manager's enemies.

Herzog's and my different choices at this early stage lead to different problems and to different readings. Herzog no longer has to make, as do I, a coherent case to explain the manager's shift from competence to carelessness. He has instead obligated himself to answer different but equally difficult questions. I want here to use this example of contrasting opening moves to underscore the shared constraints under which every parable interpreter works. When filling in the narrative's early gaps, one's preliminary choices necessarily limit those options available to make sense of the remaining and also incompletely explained sequences. However one starts out, the goal remains constant. Using data that are only partially explained, parable interpreters work toward coherence.

Introducing the problem of how one decides among interpretations, Tolbert (1979:33), in some detail and with some humor, describes how different interpretations of the parables have existed from earliest times to the present: "Each interpreter arrived at interpretations of the parables that differed significantly from those of every other interpreter, whether or not they were members of the same critical school . . . independent of the type of method used . . . independent of the period or time of scholarship . . . independent of the literary sensitivity and focus of the interpreter."

What some have seen as an aberration—the many and varied interpretations of the parables—may in fact be the consequence of deliberate design. I agree with those who believe (see, for example, Funk, ed., 1974) that these narratives were created to be the subject of multiple interpretations. Surely they provide no definitive support for any single understanding. Instead they appear to offer partially defined, ready repositories for our own perspectives.

A novel by Jerzy Kosinski, *Being There,* may be read as a parody on parable interpretation. An unknown man, handsome and well-dressed, suddenly appears. Being mentally deficient, he speaks seldom and elliptically. Yet his naive content is construed by others as metaphor. He is then fashioned by these others to represent a discordant mix of their own desires.

Schneiders (1993:33) writes, "Are there any criteria of validity in interpretation? How do we keep people from treating the biblical text as a Rorschach inkblot upon which they can project whatever agenda they currently carry? . . . there are criteria—such as methodological integrity, fruitfulness, consistency, explanatory power, compatibility with known data, and convergence of indices— and they must be applied in judging the validity of an interpretation . . . these criteria are not restricted to historical facticity, author's intention, or the insight of the first-century audience." (See also Schneiders 1991:164-67)

I think parable interpretations should be evaluated using at least the joint criteria of coherence and evocativeness. After attempting to make sense of what is not explained, how well does the interpreter integrate these newly expanded segments? How completely are the parable's disparate parts brought together into a smoothly flowing whole? How rich and evocative is the consequent reading? As I will propose at length, the integrative work awaiting any interpreter may approximate the integrative work confronting both the superior and subordinate characters in the parable.

4. See Crossan 1980:54-58, Tolbert 24-30, and Scott 42-51.

5. See Phillips 48-55.

6. Winnicott (1975): 307.

7. Phillips 51.

8. Herzog 241, 242.

9. Ibid., 244.

10. A reader commented here, "In those days a master could care less about feeling; he dealt with facts." Precisely! These parables are located in social structures enforcing such distance between persons that most often the feeling states of patronal clients, peasants, day laborers, and slaves no longer existed as facts requiring recognition.

11. So Bailey 99.

12. Breech 105.

13. The parable offers no insight into the reasons for these lapses in the master. Schafer (1981) outlines some of the ways in which a psychotherapist might approach such reasons: "One may say that, through analysis, disclaimed actions are narratively transformed into acknowledged or claimed actions. Claimed actions are those for which the [client] accepts some significant measure of responsibility, say, having blinded oneself to the untrustworthiness of a business associate" (4,5). Again, "more generally, the question is. . . . How has this person subjectively implicated himself or herself in an event which, in conventional terms, clearly has been suffered rather than enacted?" (5). Says Schafer, "So far as it is reasonable to do so, analysts retell these apparently passively suffered afflictions as actions performed by persons in situations that, in large measure, they have unconsciously constructed themselves" (29).

Derrett (1960-61) offers the intriguing proposition that the master's ignoring is in fact a purposive avoidance of his own participation. Derrett describes the rich man as a religiously committed person who wants not only to appear but also to feel morally upright; at the same time, however, he wants to charge religiously illegal interest on his loans. Derrett (202) then supposes a close, entwined relationship between rich man and manager in which the latter, knowing his master's conflicted desire, himself incurs the religiously reprehensible usury without the master having overtly to acknowledge his participation—either to himself or to others. Here is the world of the semi-aware, of partially denied agency, leaving it largely to the subordinate to feel the consequences of getting his hands dirty. What should be recognized here is Derrett's groundbreaking supposition that the rich man is actively contributing to the untoward behavior of his subordinate.

14. Blass and Debrunner, section 165.

15. This conclusion follows Topel (218, n. 10).

16. I here follow Derrett (1960-61:217) and Bailey (101-02).

17. A psychotherapeutic perspective would suppose the matter to be more complex than this simple cause-effect relationship between the behavior of the superior and the response of the subordinate. Such a perspective would provide for layer upon layer of interactions involving various combinations of all of the following: (1) the superior's unempathic behavior toward his subordinate; (2) the subordinate's misunderstanding of that behavior; (3) the subordinate's unempathic behavior toward the superior based on his misunderstanding of the superior's behavior; and (4) the superior's distorted response based on his failure to understand his subordinate's response. And so on.

Such a perspective would also propose that an account needs to be given of the transformations and consequent misunderstandings that take place inside a person's private imaginative world, particularly when one's efforts to be effective, because of the other's response, are overly frustrated or overly gratified.

A major premise of psychotherapy on which this book is based is both simple and extraordinarily complex: *we, as persons, become whom we are with*. This statement condenses the idea that we are social beings dependent on the response of others. Every subsequent interaction builds upon all those that have come before. We develop confidently held patterns of hopeful or fearful expectation; we learn to know in advance how others will respond to us. Relying on such expectations, we impose into the present benign or malevolent cycles of give and take. Positive expectations lead to a reciprocal widening of experience; negative expectations, by contrast, result in constricted and distorted initiatives, often provoking similar responses in turn. See, for example, Adler 68-76.

18. A psychoanalytic perspective would further assume an internal ambivalence, so that both superior and subordinate harbor conflicting points of view within themselves, one of which may be aligned with that of the other person, who opposes the conscious desires of the first. This complicated idea is explored at length in chap. 5.

19. These two sentences are from Todd Sumner.

20. These sentences are from Karen Ford.

21. So Breech 105.

Chapter 2

1. It is astonishing to realize that for centuries nearly every English translation of the two slave parables in this book has rendered the Greek word *doulos* inaccurately as "servant." Such rendering mutes the term's essential meaning in these stories, namely, that one human being retains complete control over the life choices of another. No such nicety overtakes these same translators when *doulos*

is encountered in the Pauline Epistles. There the identical Greek word frequently receives its proper meaning of "slave." Such has been the strength of this bias that it took the translators of the august *Revised Standard Version* until 1989, in their *New Revised Standard Version* to render the word *doulos* correctly as "slave." The lexicographers Arndt and Gingrich (204) put the matter succinctly: "*doulos* [means] . . . slave . . . 'servant' for 'slave' is largely confined to Biblical transl[ations] . . . in normal usage at the present time the two words are carefully distinguished."

It is easy to speculate on the reasons for this intractable translator distortion. "Servant" evokes images of paid positions within the households of the English gentry of bygone eras—images not particularly offensive. "Slave," by contrast, pushes into awareness associations far less agreeable: the complete stripping away, essential to any institutionalized slavery, of one's own control over subsistence, family integrity, and future choice. These troubling associations become more acute when, unlike the Pauline metaphor, the parable evokes the actual life circumstances of a slave. See Fortna 217, n. 15. See n. 20 below and n. 12 of chap. 3.

2. Kloppenborg (1988:200) cites the large bibliography representing the debate as to whether these versions represent separate traditions or derive from a common source. I follow those who believe the Matthean and Lukan versions probably reflect a single form that goes back to Jesus.

3. Many scholars (see, for example, Donahue 105-06; Fitzmeyer 1985:1228-33; Funk, Scott, and Butts, eds. 55, Jeremias 58-63; and Lambrecht 167-83) suppose that the editors of both Matthew and Luke altered the story line and some details of the parable. Quoting Funk, Scott, and Butts, eds. (55):

> Matthew has preserved the more original form of the parable, yet even he has modified it so as to identify the returning master with Jesus at his second coming. That is made clear by the addition of the phrase, "enter into the joy of your master," after the review of the first two servants, and the insertion of "And cast the worthless servant into the outer darkness; there men will weep and gnash their teeth" after the condemnation of the third. These phrases are associated with the final judgment. Luke has recast the parable as the story of a nobleman who petitions for a kingdom. This reflects Luke's interest in Jesus as king. . . ."
> As they also observe, Luke has interspersed a secondary story throughout the parable proper. It is located in the following sentences and fragments: "A nobleman went to a distant country to get royal power for himself and then return. But the citizens of his country hated him and sent a delegation after him, saying, 'We do not want this man to rule over us' . . . having received the royal power . . . 'of ten cities' . . . 'of five cities' . . . 'But as for these enemies of mine, who did not want me to be king over them— bring them here and slaughter them in my presence.'" (Luke 19:12, 14, 15b, 17c, 18c, 27) Z

Both versions have conclusions (Matt. 25:29, Luke 19:25-26) thought to be later additions.

4. See Herzog (160–61); Cardenal (4:39–40); Fortna (214, 218); Rohrbaugh (33, 35); and Kahler (171–79). The German words are, respectively, "unmenschlich hart" (171), "Blutsauger" (172), "Menschenschinder" (173), "Dieb" (173), "Wucherer" (173), and "Kredithaien" (179). Kahler (173-74) cites both Josephus (*Against Apion* 2: 27) and Philo (no reference given), together with biblical passages (Deuteronomy 23:20, Nehemiah 5:1-13, Psalms 15:5, Proverbs 28:8, and Ezekiel 18:8, 13, 17) to indicate how the taking of interest was, both within ancient Israel and the Israel of Jesus' era, considered a crime.

5. This paragraph is from a lecture by Esther Shapiro.

6. See Rohrbaugh 33-35. I have been greatly influenced in my understanding of this parable by the Kenyan author Ngugi wa Thiong'o. In his 1987 novel, *The Devil on the Cross,* Ngugi engages the conceit of a white colonialist entrepreneur, forced by African nationalism to flee, who entrusts both his capital and his tactics to retainer Africans, who in turn become subordinate but no less sophisticated exploiters. Ngugi (84-85) then has the "last slave" challenge this entire system as follows: "You, lord and master, member of the white race, I have discovered your tricks! I have also discovered your real name, Imperialist, that's your real name, and you are a cruel master. Why? Because you reap where you have never sown. You grab things over which you have never shed any sweat. You have appointed yourself the distributor of things which you have never helped to produce. Why? Just because you are the owner of capital. And so I went and buried your money in the ground to see if your money would yield anything without being fertilized by my sweat or that of any other man. Behold, here is your 100,000 shillings, exactly as you left it."

This brief summary and the quote to which I am limited cannot but hint at Ngugi's extraordinary insights. His entire novel, for which this parable forms a centerpiece, can be read as a commentary on it. In part because of his masterful use of irony, I find Ngugi's to be the most effective response to a parable of Jesus I have ever encountered. He painfully explores the constraints and consequent corruption pressing in on any Third World nationalism attempting to transform the overwhelming intrusion of Western imperialism. In so doing, I believe he rightly senses the limits with which the parable surrounds the options open to this last slave. The ironic brilliance of Ngugi's approach adds to my conviction that one of the best places to discover powerful understandings of Jesus' parables is in the Third World. See Fortna 216. (For awareness of Ngugi's work, I am indebted to Karen Ford.)

7. See Carney 63, 90, 92-94, 101, 171, 250, and 337, partly cited by Crossan (1991):59.

8. Carney 250; see also 99–101, 198–200.

9. A consensus among scholars now replaces "B.C." ("Before Christ") and "A.D." ("*Anno Domini*" or "The Year of Our Lord") with the more neutral "B.C.E." ("Before the Common Era") and "C.E." ("Common Era").

10. For the contents of this paragraph, see Freyne, 1994:116-21 and Horsley (1996a: 215-21).

11. For the contents of this paragraph see Crossan (1991:16-19) and Horsley (1996B:43-51). Yeivin (19) cites Josephus (*Jewish Antiquities* 14:5,4; *Jewish War* 1:8,5), as reporting that one of the five Jewish sanhedrins, or high courts, was assigned to Sepphoris in 55 B.C.E. and remained there until the late 60s C.E.

12. Horsley (1996b): 30.

13. Josephus, *Jewish Antiquities* 17:271.

14. See Horsley (1996b): 32, 50; Josephus, *Jewish Antiquities* 18:27.

15. Meier 407.

16. Among the tools available at that time were "the hammer, mallet, chisel, saw, hatchet, ax, adz, gimlet, drill, knife, plane, rasp, lathe, the square, straight-edge and ruler, chalk line, plumb line, level, and compasses." (Meier 311, n. 156 citing Furfey 209)

17. I do not understand why scholars seem to resist this possibility. Perhaps they are interested in segregating Jesus from the presumed—although probably superficial (see Horsley 1996B: 57-60)—Hellenistic influences of Sepphoris. Certainly the over-taxed peasants of the surrounding villages hated the over-privileged power-brokers of Sepphoris (see Horsley 1996B: 111–12, 123–25). However—as with today's Palestinians constructing Israeli settlements—such hostility would not have prevented the resident artisans tasked with rebuilding Sepphoris from needing help, nor a rural artisan like Jesus from walking four miles to seek employment.

18. Meshorer 160–61; Josephus, *Jewish War* 3:2, 4.

19. See Josephus, *Life* 8:67, cited in Freyne 1994:119. One may suppose one of their main goals was the burning of their debt records (So Crossan, personal communication).

20. The range of meanings of "slave" in Paul's letters is in marked contrast to the usage suggested here. For Paul, "slave" is a highly specific term embedded in a complex metaphorical tour de force. Paul gives the term his special significance by making it one polarity in a series of mirror opposites: son vs. slave, firstborn vs. slave-master (or Lord), life vs. death, and non-believing Jew vs. believing non-Jew. (I owe this understanding to Norman Petersen.) See Mack 1995:116.

21. By contrast, illustrating Jesus' profound engagement with his Jewish tradition, see the Appendix: "Two Sons and a Father [The Prodigal Son] and the Book of Genesis."

22. Derrett (1965:191), who makes quite another use of it, is the first commentator I know to recognize "the sauciness of his speech . . . [that] both upbraids and defies."

23. A slightly different version of this position is proposed by Rohrbaugh, 36.

24. Winnicott (1975): 208, 209.

25. This quote is from Stephen Bishop.

26. For masterful accounts of just such strategies among slaves in the United States, see Osofsky (passim) and Raboteau, chap. 6, "Religion, Rebellion, and Docility." (I owe this latter reference to Karen Ford.)

27. Fortna 226.
28. Crossan (1994): 154.

Chapter 3

1. Matthew 18:35 reads: "So also my heavenly Father will do to every one of you, if you do not forgive your brother from your heart." Many scholars (for example, Funk, Scott, and Butts, eds., 49, 106) believe the editor of Matthew authored this verse. See n. 4 below.

2. See chap. 2, n. 1. It is clear that in the present parable the master is in complete control of the life decisions of this subordinate; the latter is thus placed firmly in the social category of slave.

3. DeBoer's layout has the advantage of making obvious what is sometimes difficult to see, namely, the parallel between what the slave does ("threw him into prison") and what the master finally does ("handed him over to the jailers"). The master cannot break out of the pattern he expects his slave to escape.

In his revision of this text, DeBoer argues that the editor of the Gospel of Matthew has changed important elements of the parable better to fit a later theological perspective. The parable in its received form presents the listener with the jarring fact that a slave owes a king an impossibly large sum of money, namely, "ten thousand talents." One talent is estimated as the equivalent of fifteen years' wages for a day laborer (*New Revised Standard Version*, note for Matt. 18:24). Ten thousand talents, therefore, would amount to possibly eighteen million dollars. (It is sometimes suggested that a characteristic of Jesus' parables is exaggeration and hyperbole. Rarely, however, is evidence offered other than this present purported circumstance.)

DeBoer hypothesizes that the editor of Matthew has inflated the amount of the loan by shifting one word: from an original "ten thousand *denarii*" (a day laborer's wage for perhaps 27 years) to "ten thousand *talents*." DeBoer argues that before one can appreciate fully the reason for this revision one must entertain the added possibility that the Matthean editor has shifted the first of six uses of the word *kyrios* ("master") into *basileus* ("king"). This shift in turn encourages one further revision: the editor changes the slave's probable *parekalei* ("was beseeching") into the more appropriate *prosekynei* ("was worshiping"). (The Greek *daneion* simply means "loan" and not "debt.") DeBoer proposes that the Matthean editor's intent is to impel the listener to interpret the parable allegorically and to understand the king/master as a figure for God.

(For a second example of Matthew's apparent willingness to revise what probably was a more original version of a parable, see Crossan's [1985:46-49] discussion of the Great Supper.)

If one accepts the figure of 10,000 denarii, other elements of the story fall into place. (One denarius was the daily wage for a laborer.) DeBoer writes (228): "The sum of 10,000 denarii . . . is conceivable as a loan (v 27). The master of the parable could reasonably hope to recover such a loan, or a good portion of it, from the sale of the servant and his household (v 25), since, according to Jeremias, 'the average value of a slave was about 500 to 2,000 denarii. . . .'

"Similarly, he could hope to recover this amount from the servant's relatives and friends (as Derrett suggests) upon throwing the servant into prison "until he should pay everything that was owed" (v 34).

"Furthermore, the sum of 10,000 denarii is large enough to make the servant's difficulty in paying up plausible (v 26a), yet small enough to make his plea for patience and his promise to repay the whole amount credible (v 26b). And finally, the sum is substantial enough to provide an appropriate contrast with the still much smaller though hardly trivial sum owed by the fellow servant in v 28."

4. DeBoer's reasons for understanding this verse as a Matthean addition may be summarized as follows (see 219-21): (1) the term "brother" (Greek: *adelphos*), which appears in this verse and elsewhere in Matthew but not in the parable proper, evidently designates a specific grouping within the Matthean Christian community; (2) the phrase "my heavenly Father" is specifically Matthean. There are seventeen instances of "my Father," "my heavenly Father," or "my Father in heaven" in Matthew. The latter two phrases are unique to Matthew; (3) The warning of Matt. 6:15, unique to Matthew, anticipates 18:35: "But if you do not forgive people their trespasses, neither will your Father forgive your trespasses."

5. DeBoer 221.

6. Crossan (1973:107) is alone among the commentators to observe this "sheer stupidity." Yet he does not go on to explore its significance.

7. This paragraph in part is from Allen Comstock.

8. Carney (214) describes the various levels of slavery available as options for this master: "Slavery assumed a variety of forms in the course of antiquity. Slavery on a plantation or in the mines was unspeakably the worst of these. Being born into a household, or being acquired, for one's expertise, to serve the business affairs of a great household, was probably the 'best.' Working to pay to buy oneself out of slavery was possibly a 'good' intermediate type of slavery."

9. For a detailed and painful exploration of just this problem among the defeated slave-masters of the U.S. Civil War, see Roark's *Masters Without Slaves*, especially 196-209. (I owe this reference to Karen Ford.)

10. Schafer (1981):6.

11. Scott 272.

12. A comparable example of what, to the modern eye, appears as an ancient slave-master's amazing inability to acknowledge the effects of his control over another human being while at the same time expressing great affection for him can be found in a series of letters from the Roman aristocrat Cicero to his slave and confidant Tiro, quoted in Crossan (1991:48-50). For a potent commentary on this proposed dilemma facing the master, see Petersen's study of Paul's *Letter to Philemon*, especially pages 287-302. For another, quite different perspective, richly suggestive for this parable, see Kojeve on Hegel's master/slave dialectic, especially pages 45-56.

13. The following two paragraphs are derived from Winnicott 1965:15-28.

14. Winnicott (1965): 16.

15. Readers unfamiliar with this kind of psychological thinking may be helped by seeing it as a partial explanation of why, for example, an abused child placed in a foster home cannot readily accept affection and caring. For such a child, if he has not withdrawn completely, felt anger and hate represent his safest ways of coming close to important others. Love and forgiveness, on the other hand, provoke in him terror, since such attitudes threaten loss of the only ways of relating he has ever known.

16. For one of the most sensitive commentaries on slavery to survive antiquity (written by an aristocrat), see Letter 47 (Hooper 62-65, quoting Campbell) of Lucius Annaeus Seneca (c. 4 B.C.E.–65 C.E.). For descriptions of slavery in the ancient Mediterranean world, see Crossan (1991: chap. 3), Carney (102-103, 214-15), and Bartchy.

17. For much of the remainder of this section I am indebted to Carol Pepper. Although what follows uses the assumptions, setting, and vocabulary of psychotherapy, the processes described are not, of course, limited to psychotherapy.

18. This simplified exposition bypasses many complications. For example, sometimes the one being hurt (the therapist) transforms herself into the one doing the hurting. A shifting series of interactions may occur in which both therapist and client hurt, are hurt, make repairs, and accept those repairs. Another complexity is that these two "persons" may either be understood as real, that is, contemporary and interpersonal, or they may be understood as representations of past experience. In this latter mode, both client and therapist are reenacting how the client once experienced significant others and how those others affected him.

19. This paragraph summarizes Winnicott 1975:207-209.

20. See Stolorow 220.

21. The subtleties of unilateral coercion hidden within the master's query, "Was it not necessary also for you to have mercy on your fellow slave, as I had mercy on you?" are brought into relief when contrasted with a portion of the Lord's Prayer, "Forgive us our debts, as we also have forgiven our debtors" (Matt. 6:12). In the former, generosity is discovered in a context of control; in the latter, entreaty is discovered in a context of both needfulness and generosity. It may be that the ability to be forgiven emanates primarily from the capacity to forgive, which in turn develops out of an awareness of lack. Put another way, how would the master (or slave) need to change to be able to articulate this portion of the Lord's Prayer? (I owe these observations to John Ford.) Compare *Ecclesiasticus* [also called the *Wisdom of Jesus Son of Sirach*, written sometime before 180 B.C.E.] 28:2: "Forgive your neighbor the wrong he has done, and then your sins will be pardoned when you pray.")

22. For another compelling psychodynamic description of the origins and vicissitudes of aggression apt for the exploration of this parable, see Kohut 111-31, especially 124-25.

Chapter 4

1. "A lacuna in the papyrus makes the Coptic here uncertain; the hole might be filled in to read either 'good person' or 'usurer'" (Miller, ed., 316). I choose the former reading, as it clearly fits with my understanding of the parable.

2. Charlesworth (Weaver and Charlesworth, eds., 55, 61, n. 23) insists, accurately, that the Coptic here reads, "Perhaps he did not know them." By taking the focus off the tenants' increasing obtuseness, the Coptic inexplicably frustrates the normal story-telling strategy of a triple repetition leading to a climax. I have therefore followed those who assume copier error.

3. Appended to this parable, in verses 6-8, is commentary purportedly spoken by Jesus. I follow those who believe these verses are part of a later tradition. See, for example, Funk, Scott, and Butts, eds., 41, 106. Drury (1985:153) suggests that the Lukan editor's understanding of this parable is derived from *Ecclesiasticus* (also called the *Wisdom of Jesus Son of Sirach*) 35:13-18.

4. This translation of the Coptic of *Thomas* 65 is from Funk, Scott, and Butts, eds. 51. I have, however, changed "servant" to "slave," assuming, as do scholars regularly, that the Coptic is a translation of the Greek *doulos* (as the word appears in all three of the extant Greek versions). See chap. 2, n.1.

This parable exists in four versions: Mark 12:1b-8, Matthew 21:33b-39, Luke 20:9b-15, and *Thomas* 65. I have chosen the account found in the *Gospel of Thomas*. An extensive debate exists in the literature as to which, if any, of these four versions may be considered the more original. Part of the discussion, narrowly defined, turns on whether the more abbreviated form in *Thomas* represents (1) an earlier version, prior to the accretion of allegorical elements of interest to the early church [so, for example, Crossan 1971:451-65; idem, 1985:37, 53-62; Funk, Scott, and Butts, eds. 50-51, 98-99; and Stroker 98 100] or (2) a later stripping away of those same elements in support of the Thomas editor's interest in gnosticism [so, for example, Snodgrass 41-71; and Meier 123-39]. Scott (237-45) offers a comprehensive review of the problem.

To support my own selection of the *Thomas* version as the more original, I have placed it side by side with the single available version of a Widow and a Judge found in Luke 18:2b-5. Throughout the next two chapters I invite the reader to evaluate the resonances between these two stories and then decide whether the *Thomas* account is more likely than the allegorized versions found in Mark, Matthew, and Luke to be the product of the imagination that created a Widow and a Judge.

Charlesworth (1988:138-56) proposes that the historical Jesus (as author of the parable) may be assigning to himself the position of the parable's son. Such an assumption—that particular historical events underlie these narratives— runs counter to the entire tenor of this book.

5. Scott 252.

6. For a sensitive description of the dilemmas facing even the most empathic of landlords when confronting his landless tenant farmer, see Berry 76-84.

7. On the other hand, progress in psychotherapy also requires that the therapist, joined slowly by the client, provide an attitude of steady curiosity sufficiently unperturbed by client efforts to preserve safety through rejecting and distracting behaviors.

8. Burdened with a desire to ascribe lawfulness to someone, listeners often turn to the widow. Assuming that she lacks influence or power, one is tempted to impute justice to her unnamed cause. Yet the parable offers no evidence that the widow's intention is just; equally plausible is the inference that she is trying to compel the judge to tyrannize a victim. So, for example, Hedrick (198-99), who supposes that the widow is after vengeance and "wants her opponent to suffer."

9. See, for example, Funk, Scott, and Butts, eds., passim, and, for these two parables, 41 and 50–51.

10. Nor is any resolution discovered by understanding this parable to be an allegory about Jesus' murder—an understanding, in turn, that has had the horrific effect of contributing to Christian anti-Semitism.

11. The therapist's role, however, is to refuse such an assignment. (See, for example, chap. 2 in Gardner.) Having agreed to enter into the client's imaginative world, the therapist agrees both not to know what to do and not to be put off by not knowing. She agrees because she understands that the client's not knowing has come about for crucial, even lifesaving reasons. If the therapist believes that she from the outside can know what to do, she avoids intimate contact with the costly but substantial reasons for the client's earlier not knowing. The client, in turn, can emerge from his anxiety only by entering into these reasons, which effort first requires that the therapist achieve some feeling conviction of what it was like to be this client. A seasoned therapist captured this process with the following metaphor: "It is as if two people agree to climb into the same prison cell; then together they try to find a way out" (Otto Allen Will, Jr.).

Chapter 5

1. For this and the following paragraph I am indebted to Michels 13-14. *For the phrase "patterns of expectation" as a way of capturing the psychoanalytic concept of transference, I am indebted to Basch (1980:35).

2. The feeling states aroused in the psychotherapist by the client's transferences are one aspect of what is termed "countertransference." Such countertransference is understood as a major source of information in any ongoing psychotherapy.

3. I have been aided in this perception by Schafer, 1997.

4. This paragraph is from a discussion with Carol Pepper.

Perhaps the most significant gap (or absence of explanation, requiring listener surmise) in this parable is found here, namely, in the judge's determined and lengthy delay when responding to the widow's demand. The listener must first supply some hypotheses to explain why the judge delays and later must synthesize that hypothesis with an explanation for his sudden responsiveness. The reader may be interested to compare my own assumptions when filling this gap with those of two recent commentators, neither of whom relies on the Lukan reversal to understand the parable. Both Herzog (220-32) and Hedrick (193-207) are sensitive to the problems created by the judge's delay; their solutions, however, are about as far apart from each other as they are from my own.

5. When describing the judge, I have been experimenting with a therapist assumption that one can infer the other's childhood experience from one's feeling response to the other's current behavior. Clearly, however, there are instances—and the widow's is one of them—where adolescent or adult trauma so infiltrates contemporary experience that inferences about childhood history are unwarranted. With this character, then, I limit my exploration to the suggestion that the widow's adult experience may be analogous to that of a child with its parents.

6. See Alice Miller 1981: chap. 3.

7. Shapiro and Carr's description (24–25, derived from Zimmer).

8. I have adapted these four steps from Shapiro and Carr's eight steps (24). For a lucid outline of this complex concept, called "projective identification," see Shapiro and Carr 22-34. For a definitive exposition, see Grotstein.

9. So Milavec (1990:32), who makes a different use of it: "Any prudent owner of an estate would have sent a sizable armed guard with his son, but not this one."

Chapter 6

1. Breech 184–212.

2. Breech, 190.

3. E.g., Bornkamm 126–27; Crespy 242; Bailey 161–62.

4. Bailey 161–62.

5. *King Lear,* Act I, Scene 2.

6. *Metamorphoses*, Book II, lines 51–55, 102–13 (King, trans. 335–37).

7. Derrett (1970): 108-09. For the previous paragraph, see Derrett (1970): 107-11. Derrett (1970:109, n. 1) cites later mishnaic law: "The law is stated plainly at B.B. VII.7 . . : 'If a man assigned his property in writing to his son (for) after his death, the father cannot sell it since it is assigned (or written) to the son, and the son cannot sell it because it is within the . . . dominion [or] absolute control . . . of the father. If the father sold it, it is sold until he dies; if the son sold it the purchaser has no claim until the father dies.'" Derrett believes that this (late second century C.E.) mishnaic law "fits the situation described in our parable."

8. Khan, 226.

9. Blos (1985): 32.

10. Blos (1985): 142. Readers may be as enthralled as I was to follow the implications of this statement by Blos into an understanding of this parable provided by a twelve-year-old young man. In the illustrations that follow, David draws and then comments upon his realization, albeit outside his awareness, that

the father does for the son what unconsciously he wants the son to do for him, namely, provide and nurture. (Compare here Scott [122], who describes the first half of this process: "The father combines in himself the maternal and paternal roles. As a father he is a failure, but as a mother he is a success.")

David's understanding is compelling both in its explicitness and in the subtleties of its sequence. With powerful imaginative strokes, made persuasive by the gradualness of their development, David first perceives the father as a pregnant mother—or, in his explanation, as Santa Claus—the one who provides without expectation of return.

David then imagines the younger son using his father's money to have himself transformed into the beginnings of one who will later nurture, namely, a prepubescent girl. At the nadir of the son's resourcelessness and under the aegis of the father's renewed largess, David then conceives the young man's final and disastrous transformation: the boy is now a well-endowed, abundantly providing adult woman. The younger son has become a nurturing mother/wife.

David's sketch, originally drawn with felt-tip pens on a five-foot sheet of paper laid on the floor, is here reproduced in miniature along with his later commentary. On subsequent pages significant aspects of his drawing are enlarged.

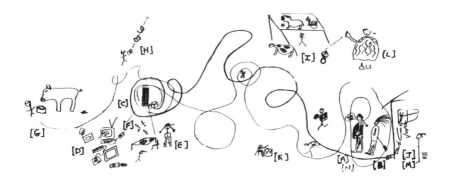

David C.'s Commentary on A Father and Two Sons

A. This is the father and the [elder] son. Watching the one who goes away.

B. That guy has an arrow up his butt. I don't know why he has an arrow up his butt. Actually, it's in his back.

C. He buys a skyscraper from the town.

D. He buys all this expensive stuff. Electronics mostly.

E. He has money. So he gets a sex change operation. I don't know why. He has two pigtails. With his cowboy boots on.

F. He invites all his friends over.

G. He spends all his money. He has to feed the pigs. And he loses all his hair. And he eats the pig stuff.

H. He travels home. There's the money flying away.

I. He gets all his presents because his father likes that he's back after a long journey.

J. And his brother thinks that's bad. He's been working for his father and he doesn't get the fatted cow and presents.

K. They have music players.

L. Then he gets a big dress. No a big robe thing. [David's teacher drew the feet, head, and arms.]

M. That's his brother coming in from the fields.

N. I drew a big belly on him, the dad, and he's saying "Ho, Ho, Ho." He looks like Santa Claus. Santa Claus is fat. That's a stereotype.

A. This is the father and the [elder] son. Watching the one who goes away.

B. That guy has an arrow up his butt. I don't know why he has an arrow up his butt. Actually, it's in his back.

N. I drew a big belly on him, the dad, and he's saying "Ho, Ho, Ho." He looks like Santa Claus. Santa Claus is fat. That's a stereotype.

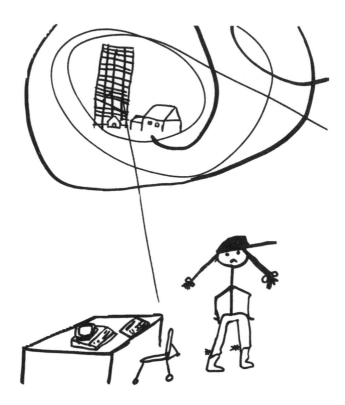

C. He buys a skyscraper from the town.

D. He buys all this expensive stuff. Electronics mostly.

E. He has money. So he gets a sex-change operation. I don't know why. He has two pigtails. With his cowboy boots on.

L. Then he gets a big dress. No a big robe thing. [David's teacher drew the feet, head, and arms.]

11. Breech (204) (apart from a brief observation by Koester [1992:10]) is the only commentator I know to emphasize the failure of the father to set limits: "[The father] responds spontaneously to indulge the son whose existence is characterized by voracious wanting. Having that son with him excites him and he behaves in accordance with the excitement he feels. He prefers the excitement to maintaining any standards as a father. Indeed, from this perspective he cannot be said to live as a 'father.'"

Breech, however, does not develop this ground-breaking insight. He does not infer from the father's lack of limits a provocation of the younger son's voraciousness. He tends to treat the dyad of father and younger son as composed of two separate persons rather than as an interacting unit where the son's actions are intimately reactive to those of the father. Breech sees the younger son's self-indulgence as distinct from what the father first does. (Later, however, when describing how the father's inability to listen is directly responsible for the angry response of his elder son, Breech [204] adopts an explicitly interactive model.)

12. Blos (1967): 167.

13. Blos (1985): 138.

14. Breech (192) observes that the original meaning of the Greek word *asotos,* translated as "dissolute living," is "incurably ill." "The younger son was acting in so self-indulgent a way that he could be described as someone who is incurably ill."

15. See, for example, Fairbairn (109-15).

16. Breech 193.

17. Breech (198) is the only interpreter I know who makes this point. "The story discloses that when the son was independent of [the father], not wanting things from him, he was non-existent. In other words, the son is alive to the man only when he uses his father."

18. See Scott, 117; Entrevernes Group, 166–67.

19. Schafer, a contemporary psychoanalyst, suggests that to the classic historical question, What happened? there are a number of legitimate answers rather than one. To illustrate his point he provides an example from psychoanalytic practice that inadvertently supplies a complex introduction to the possible meanings lodged in this parable between father and son: "The same significant action gets told many times during an analysis. The action is brought up in, or is reassigned to, different contexts. For example, a father's seductiveness may sometimes be told in a context from which it emerges as parental overstimulation and sometimes in a context from which it emerges as a reliable, even if difficult, experience of parental interest that stands in contrast to the experience of maternal animosity or neglect; at yet other times, the context of the seductiveness may be parental discord, the mother getting to be seen depressed and the father as turning desperately to the child for some kind of love; and finally its context may be the child's own seductiveness toward the overeager father, perhaps as rivalrous move on the child's part divide the parents" (1981:40-41).

Chapter 7

1. Herzog (82-83) gives a concise summary of the debates about whether to include any or all of verses 14-16; I follow Herzog in having the parable end with verse 15.

2. This quote is from Michelle Freemer.

3. Kahn 226.

4. This paragraph is from Carol Pepper.

5. This paragraph comes from a discussion with Carol Pepper.

6. "The elder son seems to believe, through his silent toiling to fulfill his image of an ideal son, that somehow he will cause a fundamental change in his father" (David Garfield). The elder son may well feel safe in demanding that which, out of awareness, he is certain is unavailable. What might happen were he to lose such an unconsciously protecting obstacle? Perhaps, being no longer free merely to complain, he might for the first time have the opportunity to confront the anxiety of taking his own risks.

7. See Blos (1985:32–36) for a moving clinical illustration in which a client, after great effort, achieves this freedom.

8. I am indebted in my understanding of Laborers and a Landowner both to the insights of Kaylor (129-37) and to the researches of Herzog (79-97). It was Kaylor (134) who first alerted me to the possible play between "what is lawful" and "what is just." I indicate particular points of indebtedness in the text. My own contribution is (1) an emphasis on the owner's conflicted need for honor, that is, for recognition from his workers, paralleling the need in the father to be needed, and (2) my exploring the resonances between the anger of the disenfranchised, deprived laborers and the anger of the enfranchised, deprived elder son.

9. Herzog 85.

10. See Kaylor 129, 132, 134; Herzog 94.

11. Kittel, ed., IV, 182.

12. Kittel, ed., IV, 185.

13. For the possibility that Jesus could speak Greek, see Funk (1982:19-28) and Porter (1994).

14. See Herzog 88; Carney 250.

15. Herzog 90. Oakman (1987:36-37) calculates that one denarius (a silver coin about the size of a dime) would supply an adequate energy level to an agricultural worker for three days (estimating 3,000 calories per day). This baseline estimate omits the additional facts of sporadic employment, feeding a family, paying for other needs, and a probable 30 to 40 percent level of taxation. (For this last, see Hoehner 79 and Borg 1994:103.) See also Herzog 86 and Horsley 1996a: 216-21.

16. Herzog 86, 88.

17. See Herzog 86.

18. See Kaylor 134–36.

19. Kaylor 133.

20. Latin American liberation theology understands that in elitist societies there are charitable persons, but since the entire system is unjust, there can in fact be no charity. Thus the slogan, "No justice, no charity!" (I owe this observation to Carol Pepper.)

21. Herzog 92.

22. See Herzog, 91–93.

23. This sentence is from Allen Comstock.

24. This paragraph is from Carol Pepper.

Chapter 8

1. See, for example, Miller (1981), chap. 3, "The Vicious Circle of Contempt."

2. Crossan (1975, chap. 2).

3. For a useful introduction to irony in literature, see Muecke.

4. It seems to me that a telling critique of the kind of parable allegorizing required to render the superior character a Messiah-figure or God-figure is how invariably it occurs at the expense of the parable's subordinate character. Would a leader so identified with the under-classes as was Jesus keep on making his points by using them as foils? A major question facing those who allegorize this way is, I think, whether one can gain status for the assumed Messiah-figure or God-figure (always the superior character) by denying reason for the subordinate's compromised responses to the superior's compromised initiatives.

5. For background to this debate, see Borg (1994a) and Telford. For a summary of the current debate, see Chilton. For two contemporary perspectives representing the wide range of positions taken on this issue, see Borg (1994b:47-96) and Meier (1994: 237-506, especially 450-54). For a brief summary of the fate of apocalyptic across Paul and the four canonical Gospels, see Fredriksen (62-63).

6. For a more broadly based confirmation of this perspective, see Borg (1995b:80-84).

7. Eiseley (73) has garnered this magnificent quote from an unknown fifteenth-century Christian mystic: "Heaven ghostly, is as high down as up, and up as down: behind as before, before as behind, on one side as another. Insomuch, that whoso had a true desire for to be at heaven, then that same time he were in heaven ghostly. For the high and the next way thither is run by desires and not by paces of feet."

8. I am impressed by the largely ahistorical character of these parables; they do not appear to be tied strongly to any specific milieu. Instead they represent the inevitable social inequalities, the necessary social interdependencies, and the consequent interpersonal misperceptions characteristic of all human experience. They are accounts that evoke the attention and intervention of every listener in

every age. They are stories for every place and every time.

Adoption of this ahistorical perspective does not, of course, imply a disinterest in locating these narratives within the larger context of the historical works and words of Jesus. I see these parables as representative of Jesus' invitation to an inclusive perspective— which in turn is at the heart of a profound revolution in religious symbolism that he engendered within the particularisms of first century, Hellenized Jewish Galilee. (See below, n. 11.)

9. Atwood (434).

10. For this third step, I am indebted to a discussion with Karen Ford.

11. See Chasseguet-Smirgel, chap. 1.

12. I believe the breakdown of collaboration represented in these parables between interdependent unequals is a mirror opposite of the collaboration described in the Gospel of Luke between interdependent equals. In Luke 10:2-11, Jesus sends itinerant healers into peasant villages. The healers carried no knapsacks, that is, no food. Such lack, observes Crossan (1994b:156), represents their openly expressed dependency; those householders who welcomed them acknowledged an equivalent but contrasting dependency. The providing itinerants received food and a place to sleep; the providing householders received healing. Here is reciprocity, a give and take among equals across difference. Neither group can function without the other; both become capable as a consequence of their fitted lack. Crossan identifies such collaboration as "the atomic unit of the Jesus movement."

Compare this description of collaboration among differing equals with the parables' portrayal of a generosity or power that denies any corresponding need to receive.

(I am indebted to Freyne [1988:219-68] for parts of the following argument.) Jesus was executed, I believe, not simply because he challenged the economic injustices of either the Temple aristocracy or Imperial Rome, but because, by including everyone, he bypassed their authority; he relieved such elites of their exclusive access, through ritual purity or military power, to the divine. Jesus' compassionate inclusion of everyone eventually undermines those particularisms of Judaism that require the exclusion of the dead nations of the Gentiles, those particularisms of Rome that require the exclusion of the expendable poor, and those particularisms of Christianity that require the exclusion of any who do not believe in the Christ. (Compare Crossan [1988B:11-12]).

I think the parables here studied undermine the exclusionary propensities of any and every hierarchy, be it based on economics, politics, military power, intellectual achievement, apocalyptic (Day of Judgment) expectations, age, gender, ethnicity, or religion. They infiltrate and collapse any ascendency of the included that requires the exclusion of others. They do so by inviting listeners, who in some way already believe themselves excluded, toward the feeling or conviction of being participants in exclusionary practices similar to those they have up until now been opposing.

13. Some believe that a seminal parable, that is, a parable about parables, is found in the thirty-three words of the Hidden Treasure in the Field (Matthew 13:44): "The kingdom of heaven is like a treasure hidden in a field, which some-one found and hid; then in his joy he goes and sells all that he has and buys that field." Here the listener may assume that what is hidden is worth more than what is already possessed. The decisive act is to discover the location of what is hid-den. Once one finds that place, all other decisions, however unethical (see Crossan, 1979, 90-93), flow from that discovery.

Irony resides within this perspective. The actions that follow readily from the uncovering of what is hidden may themselves result in novel positions of control. At last in possession, we may be enticed away from the uncertainty and wonder-ing that further discovery requires. The very processes leading to novelty may later function to close it out; opening up may result in shutting down. (This para-graph is from Todd Sumner.)

Perhaps we must be content to pass on to the next generation those discover-ies that have become our controlling possessions. They in their turn may be able once again to break open the novel hidden within the familiar. One attends with renewed interest to the efforts in these parables of one person to give into the hands of another that which she or he has first wrested into possession. And one returns, sobered but eager, to the present task of how, in this generation, to attend once more to these stories—"once more," to use the apt title of a book on the parables, "to be astonished." (Lambrecht, 1983).

14. I understand that Mark 10:15 may be translated as "Whoever does not receive the Kingdom of God as if it were (*hos*) a child. . . ." See Arndt and Gin-grich (906): "*hos* [can] introduce the characteristic quality of a per[son], thing, or action . . . [for example] . . . 'why am I still being condemned as a sinner?' Ro. 3:7."

15. The Greek phrase *entos hymon* "may mean 'within you, in your hearts' . . . though many prefer to transl[ate] 'among you, in your midst.'" Arndt and Gingrich (269).

Appendix

1. This appendix has profited from a critique by Todd Sumner.

2. See Abrahams 1917:11, cited in Scott 112, n. 40), Derrett (1967:68-69; idem, 1970: 116-21), Drury (1985:145-46; 1987:433), and Scott (111-12).

3. See, for example, Friedman (87), who, after a lengthy summary of evidence (61-86), determines that the author of the J strand of Genesis lived in the south-ern kingdom of Judah sometime between 848 and 722 B.C.E. and that the author of the E strand of Genesis lived in the northern kingdom of Israel sometime between 922 and 722 B.C.E.

4. See Davies (1982:13, following von Rad) "According to von Rad, the whole of the Hexateuch in all its vast complexity was governed by the theme of

the fulfillment of the promise to Abraham in the settlement Canaan . . . von Rad holds that it the work of the Yahwist [i.e., the author of the 'J' strand of Genesis] to fuse the whole complex of the patriarchal sagas together: for him, the entry into Palestine under Joshua is the fulfillment of the promise. Later modifications of this basic pattern of J and E, in von Rad's view, were trivial. Of all the promises made to the patriarchs, it was that of The Land that was most prominent and decisive. It was the linking together of the promise to the patriarchs with the fulfillment of it in the settlement that gives to the Hexatuech its distinctive theological character. For the Hexateuch, The Land is a promised land, and that inviolably." See also Plaut 1300.

    5. See Plaut 274

    6. This sentence is from Todd Sumner.

    7. Crossan 1975:51.

    8. Crossan 1980:58.

    9. Crossan 1980:67.

Bibliography

Abrahams, Israel. 1924. *Studies in Pharisaism and the Gospels.* Second Series. Cambridge, England: Cambridge University Press. (Reprinted by the Library of Biblical Studies. New York: Ktav, 1967.)

Adler, Gerald. 1985. *Borderline Psychopathology and Its Treatment.* New York: Jason Aronson.

Alter, Robert. 1981. *The Art of Biblical Narrative.* New York: Basic Books.

_____. 1985. "Scripture and Culture." *Commentary* 2 (August): 42-48.

Applebaum, Shimon. 1976. "Economic Life in Palestine." In *The Jewish People in the First Century: Historical Geography, Political History, Social, Cultural and Religious Life and Institutions.* Compendium rerum iudaicarum ad Novum Testamentum. Edited by S. Safrai and M. Stern in cooperation with D. Flusser and W. C. van Unnik. Vol 2. Philadelphia: Fortress. 631-700.

Arndt, William F., and F. Wilbur Gingrich. 1957. *A Greek-English Lexicon of the New Testament and Other Early Christian Literature.* Chicago: University of Chicago Press.

Atwood, Margaret. 1989. *Cat's Eye.* New York: Bantam Books.

Bailey, Kenneth E. 1976. *Poet and Peasant and Through Peasant Eyes. A Literary-Cultural Approach to the Parables in Luke.* Grand Rapids, Mich.: Eerdmans.

Bartchy, S. Scott. 1973. *First-Century Slavery and the Interpretation of I Corinthians 7:21.* Society of Biblical Literature Dissertation Series. Atlanta: Scholars Press.

Barth, Marcus. 1979. "The Dishonest Steward and His Lord. Reflections on Luke 16:1-13." In *From Faith to Faith. Essays in Honor of Donald G. Miller.* Dikran Y. Hadidian, ed. Pittsburgh: Pickwick Press.

Basch, Michael Franz. 1980. *Doing Psychotherapy.* New York: Basic Books.

_____. 1988. *Understanding Psychotherapy.* New York: Basic Books.

_____. 1992. *Practicing Psychotherapy.* New York: Basic Books.

Beardslee, William A. 1980. "Listening to the Parables of Jesus. An Exploration of the Uses of Process Theology in Biblical Interpretation." In *Texts and Testaments. Critical Essays on the Bible and Early Church Fathers.* W. Eugene March, ed. San Antonio: Trinity University Press. 201-18.

Beinnaert, Louis. 1978. "The Parable of the Prodigal Son (Luke 15:11-32) Read by an Analyst." In *Exegesis: Problems of Method and Exercises in Reading (Genesis 22 and Luke 15).* Francois Bovon and Gregoire Rouiller, eds. Pittsburgh: Pickwick Press. 197-210.

Berry, Wendell. 1974. *The Memory of Old Jack.* New York: Harcourt Brace Jovanovich.

Blass, F., and A. Debrunner. 1961. *A Greek Grammar of the New Testament and Other Early Christian Literature.* Trans. and rev. Robert W. Funk. Chicago: University of Chicago Press.

Blomberg, Craig L. 1990. *Interpreting the Parables.* Downers Grove, Ill.: InterVarsity Press.

_____. 1991. "Interpreting the Parables of Jesus. Where Are We and Where Do We Go from Here?" *Catholic Biblical Quarterly* 53: 50-78.

_____. 1994. "The Parables of Jesus: Current Trends and Needs in Research." In *Studying the Historical Jesus. Evaluations of the State of Current Research.* Bruce Chilton and Craig A. Evans, eds. Leiden, New York, Köln: E. J. Brill. 231-54.

Blos, Peter. 1967. "The Second Individuation Process of Adolescence." *The Psychoanalytic Study of the Child.* XXII. New York: International Universities Press. 162-86.

_____. 1985. *Son and Father. Before and Beyond the Oedipus Complex.* New York: Free Press.

Borg, Marcus J. 1986. "A Temperate Case for a Non-Eschatological Jesus." *Forum* 2: 81-102.

_____. 1987. *Jesus, a New Vision: Spirit, Culture, and the Life of Discipleship.* San Francisco: HarperCollins.

_____. 1994a. "Reflections on a Discipline. A North American Perspective." In *Studying the Historical Jesus. Evaluations of the State of Current Research.* Bruce Chilton and Craig A. Evans, eds. Leiden, New York, Köln: E. J. Brill. 9-32.

_____. 1994b. *Jesus in Contemporary Scholarship.* Valley Forge, Pa.: Trinity Press International.

_____. 1994c. *Meeting Jesus Again for the First Time*. San Francisco: HarperSanFrancisco.

Bornkamm, Gunther. 1960. *Jesus of Nazareth*. New York: Harper.

Borsch, F. H. 1988. *Many Things in Parables. Extravagant Stories of New Community*. Philadelphia: Fortress.

Boucher, Madeline. 1977. *The Mysterious Parables. A Literary Study*. Catholic Biblical Quarterly Monograph Series 6. Washington, D.C.: Catholic Biblical Association of America.

Breech, James. 1983. *The Silence of Jesus. The Authentic Voice of the Historical Jesus*. Philadelphia: Fortress.

Cardenal, Ernesto, ed. 1982. *The Gospel in Solentiname*. 4 vols. Maryknoll, N.Y.: Orbis Books.

Carney, Thomas F. 1975. *The Shape of the Past. Models of Antiquity*. Lawrence, Kans.: Coronado Press.

Campbell, Robin A., trans. 1963. *Seneca: Letters from a Stoic*. Baltimore: Penguin Classics.

Charlesworth, James H. 1988. *Jesus Within Judaism. New Light from Exciting Archaeological Discoveries*. New York: Doubleday.

Charlesworth, James H., and Walter P. Weaver, eds. 1994. *Images of Jesus Today*. Valley Forge, Pa.: Trinity Press International.

Chasseguet-Smirgel, Janine. 1984. *Creativity and Perversion*. New York and London: W. W. Norton.

Chatman, Seymour. 1980. *Story and Discourse. Narrative Structure in Fiction and Film*. Ithaca, N.Y.: Cornell University Press.

Chilton, Bruce. 1994. "The Kingdom of God in Recent Discussion." In *Studying the Historical Jesus. Evaluations of the State of Current Research*. Bruce Chilton and Craig A. Evans, eds. Leiden, New York, Köln: E. J. Brill. 255-80.

Cooperman, Martin. 1989. "Defeating Processes in Psychotherapy." Chapter 16 in *Psychoanalysis and Psychosis*. Ann-Louise S. Silver, ed. New York: International Universities Press.

Crespy, Georges. 1976. "Psychoanalyse et Foi." *Etudes Theologiques et Religieuses* 41: 241-51.

Crossan, John Dominic. 1971. "The Parable of the Wicked Husbandmen." *Journal of Biblical Literature* 90: 451–65.

_____. 1973. In *Parables. The Challenge of the Historical Jesus*. New York: Harper & Row.

_____. 1974a. "The Servant Parables of Jesus." *SEMEIA* 1: 17–62.

_____. 1974b. "Parable and Example in the Teaching of Jesus." *SEMEIA* 1: 63–104.

_____. 1974c. "Structuralist Analysis and the Parables of Jesus." *SEMEIA* 1: 192-221.

_____. 1974d. "A Basic Bibliography for Parables Research." *SEMEIA*, 1: 236-74.

_____. 1975. *The Dark Interval. Towards a Theology of Story.* Niles, Ill.: Argus.

_____, ed. 1977. "Polyvalent Narration: A Practice Case Study on the Parable of the Prodigal Son." *SEMEIA* 9, 1-147.

_____. 1979. *Finding Is the First Act. Trove Folktales and Jesus' Treasure Parable.* Philadelphia: Fortress, and Missoula, Mont.: Scholars Press.

_____. 1980. *Cliffs of Fall. Paradox and Polyvalence in the Parables of Jesus.* New York: Seabury.

_____. 1985. *Four Other Gospels. Shadows on the Contours of Canon.* San Francisco: Harper & Row.

_____. 1988. *The Cross That Spoke. The Origins of the Passion Narrative.* San Francisco: Harper & Row.

_____. 1991. *The Historical Jesus. The Life of a Jewish Mediterranean Peasant.* San Francisco: HarperSanFransisco.

_____. 1992. "Jesus and the Lepers." *Forum* 8: 177-90.

_____. 1994a. "The Historical Jesus in Earliest Christianity." In *Jesus and Faith. A Conversation on the Work of John Dominic Crossan.* Jeffrey Carlson and Robert A. Ludwig, eds. Maryknoll, N.Y.: Orbis Books. 1-21.

_____. 1994b. "Responses and Reflections." In *Jesus and Faith. A Conversation on the Work of John Dominic Crossan.* Jeffrey Carlson and Robert A. Ludwig, eds. Maryknoll, N.Y.: Orbis Books. 142–64.

_____. 1994c. *Jesus. A Revolutionary Biography.* San Francisco: HarperSanFrancisco.

_____. 1994d. *The Essential Jesus. Original Sayings and Earliest Images.* San Francisco: HarperSanFransisco.

_____. 1995. *Who Killed Jesus? Exposing the Roots of Anti-Semitism in the Gospel Story of the Death of Jesus.* SanFrancisco: HarperSanFransisco.

Culbertson, Philip L. 1995. *A Word Fitly Spoken. Context, Transmis-

sion, and Adoption of the Parables of Jesus. Albany: State University of New York Press.

Davies, W. D. 1982. *The Territorial Dimension of Judaism.* Berkeley: University of California Press.

_____. 1984. *Jewish and Pauline Studies.* Philadelphia: Fortress.

DeBoer, Martinus C. 1988. "Ten Thousand Talents? Matthew's Interpretation and the Redaction of the Parable of the Unforgiving Servant (Matt 18:23-35)." *Catholic Biblical Quarterly* 50: 214–32.

Deidun, Thomas. 1976. "The Parable of the Unmerciful Servant." *Biblical Theology Bulletin* 6: 203–34.

Derrett, J. Duncan M. 1960-61. "Fresh Light on St. Luke XVI. The Parable of the Unjust Steward." *New Testament Studies* 198-219.

_____. 1965. "Law in the New Testament: The Parable of the Talents and Two Logia." *Zeitschrift für die Neuetestamentliche Wissenschaftt,* 184-95.

_____. 1967. "Law in the New Testament. The Parable of the Prodigal Son." *New Testament Studies* 14: 56-74.

_____. 1970. *Law in the New Testament.* London: Darton, Longman & Todd.

Dodd, Charles D. 1961. *The Parables of the Kingdom.* New York: Charles Scribner's Sons.

Dolto, Francoise, and Gerard Severin. 1979. *The Jesus of Psychoanalysis. A Freudian Interpretation of the Gospel.* Garden City, N.Y.: Doubleday.

Donahue, John. 1988. *The Gospel in Parable. Metaphor, Narrative, and Theology in the Synoptic Gospels.* Philadelphia: Fortress.

Drury, John. 1985. *The Parables in the Gospels. History and Allegory.* New York: Crossroad.

_____. 1987. "Luke." In *The Literary Guide to the Bible.* Robert Alter and Frank Kermode, eds. Cambridge, Mass.: The Belknap Press of Harvard University Press. 418-39.

Eiseley, Loren. 1971. *The Night Country.* New York: Scribner's.

Entrevernes Group, trans. Gary Phillips. 1978. *Signs and Parables. Semiotics and Gospel Texts.* Pittsburgh Theological Monograph Series 23. Pittsburgh: Pickwick Press.

Fairbairn, W. Ronald D. 1952. *Psychoanalytic Studies of the Personality.* London, Henley, and Boston: Routledge & Kegan Paul.

Fitzmeyer, Joseph A. 1964. "The Story of the Dishonest Manager." *Theological Studies* 25: 23-42.

_____. 1985. *The Gospel According to Luke X–XXIV*. The Anchor Bible. Garden City, N.Y.: Doubleday.

Fletcher, R. 1963. "The Riddle of the Unjust Steward: Is Irony the Key?" *Journal of Biblical Literature* 82: 15-30.

Ford, Lewis S. 1978. *The Lure of God: A Biblcal Background for Process Theism*. Philadelphia: Fortress.

Fortna, Robert T. 1992 (first published in 1995). "Reading Jesus' Parable of the Talents Through Underclass Eyes." *Forum* 8: 211–28.

Fredriksen, Paula. 1988. *From Jesus to Christ. The Origins of the New Testament Images of Jesus*. New Haven and London: Yale University Press.

Freyne, Sean. 1980. *Galilee from Alexander the Great to Hadrian, 323* B.C.E. to *145* C.E. *A Study of Second Temple Judaism*. University of Notre Dame Center for the Study of Judaism and Christianity in Antiquity 5. Notre Dame, Ind.: University of Notre Dame Press.

_____. 1988. *Galilee, Jesus, and the Gospels. Literary Approaches and Historical Investigations*. Philadelphia: Fortress.

_____. 1992. "Urban-Rural Relations in First-Century Galilee: Some Suggestions from the Literary Sources." In *The Galilee in Late Antiquity*. Lee I. Levine, ed. New York: The Jewish Theological Seminary of America. Distributed by Harvard University Press, Cambridge, Mass. 75-91.

_____. 1994. "The Geography, Politics, and Economics of Galilee and the Quest for the Historical Jesus." In *Studying the Historical Jesus. Evaluations of the State of Current Research*. Bruce Chilton and Craig A. Evans, eds. Leiden, New York, Köln: E. J. Brill. 75-122.

Friedman, Richard Elliott. 1987. *Who Wrote the Bible?* New York: Summit Books.

Fuchs, Ernst. 1959. "The Parable of the Unmerciful Servant." In *Studia Evangelica 5. Texte und Untersuchungen* 73. Berlin: Academie-Verlag. 487-91.

Funk, Robert W. 1966. *Language, Hermeneutic, and the Word of God. The Problem of Language in the New Testament and Contemporary Theology*. New York: Harper & Row.

_____, ed. 1974. "A Structuralist Approach to the Parables." *SEMEIA* 1.

_____. 1982. *Parables and Presence. Forms of the New Testament Tradition*. Philadelphia: Fortress.

Funk, Robert W., Bernard Brandon Scott, and James R. Butts, eds. 1988. *The Parables of Jesus. Red Letter Edition. A Report of the Jesus Seminar*. Sonoma, Calif.: Polebridge Press.

Funk, Robert W. with Mahlon H. Smith, eds. 1991. *The Gospel of Mark. Red Letter Edition*. Sonoma, Calif.: Polebridge Press.

Funk, Robert W., Roy W. Hoover, and the Jesus Seminar. 1993. *The Five Gospels. The Search for the Authentic Words of the Historical Jesus*. New York: Macmillan.

Furfey, Paul H. 1955. "Christ as *Tekton*." *Catholic Biblical Quarterly* 17: 204-15.

Gardner, M. Robert. 1983. *Self-Inquiry*. Boston: Little, Brown and Co.

Grotstein, James S. 1985. *Splitting and Projective Identification*. New York: Jason Aronson.

Hedrick, Charles W. 1994. *Parables as Poetic Fictions. The Creative Voice of Jesus*. Peabody, Mass.: Hendrickson Publishers.

Hendrickx, Herman. 1986. *The Parables of Jesus. Studies in the Synoptic Gospels*. (Revised). San Francisco: Harper & Row.

Herzog, William R., II. 1994. *Parables as Subversive Speech. Jesus as Pedagogue of the Oppressed*. Louisville, Ky.: Westminster/ John Knox Press.

Hoehner, Harold W. 1972. *Herod Antipas*. Cambridge, England: Cambridge University Press.

The Holy Bible, New Revised Standard Version. 1989. New York: Oxford University Press.

Hooper, Finley and Matthew Schwartz. 1991. *Roman Letters. History from a Personal Point of View*. Detroit: Wayne State University Press.

Horsley, Richard A. 1996a. *Galilee. History, Politics, People*. Valley Forge, Pa.: Trinity Press International.

_____. 1996B. *Archaeology, History, and Society in Galilee*. Valley Forge, Pa.: Trinity Press International.

Hunter, Archibald M. 1960. *Interpreting the Parables*. Philadelphia: Westminster Press.

Ireland, Dennis J. 1992. *Stewardship and the Kingdom of God. An Historical, Exegetical, and Contextual Study of the Parable of the Unjust Steward in Luke 16:1-13*. Supplements to *Novum Testamentum*, LXX. Leiden, New York, Köln: E. J. Brill.

Iser, Wolfgang. 1978. *The Act of Reading. A Theory of Aesthetic Response*. Baltimore: Johns Hopkins University Press.

Jeremias, Joachim. 1972. *The Parables of Jesus*. Second Edition. Trans. S. H. Hooke. New York: Charles Scribner's Sons.

Johnson, L. T. 1982. "The Lukan Kingship Parable (Lk.19:11-27)." *Novum Testamentum* XXIV: 138-59.

Julicher, Adolf. 1888-89. *Die Gleichnesse Jesu*. 2 vols. Tubingen: J. C. B. Mohr.

Kahler, Christoph. 1995. *Jesu Gleichnesse als Poesie und Therapie. Versuch eines integrativen Zugangs sum kommunikativen Aspekt von Gleichnisse Jesu*. Tubingen: J. C. B. Mohr (Paul Siebek).

Kaylor, R. David. 1994. *Jesus the Prophet. His Vision of the Kingdom on Earth*. Louisville, Ky.: Westminster/John Knox Press.

Khan, M. Masud R. 1972. "Dread of Surrender to Resourceless Dependence in the Analytic Situation." *International Journal of Psychoanalysis* 53: 225-30.

Kee, Howard Clark. 1992. "Early Christianity in the Galilee: Reassessing the Evidence from the Gospels." In *The Galilee in Late Antiquity*. Lee L. Levine, ed. New York: The Jewish Theological Seminary of America. Distributed by Harvard University Press, Cambridge, Mass. 3-22.

King, Henry, trans. 1903. *Masterpieces of Latin Literature*. Gordon J. Laing, ed. New York: Houghton, Mifflin & Co.

Kissinger, Warren S. 1979. *The Parables of Jesus. A History of Interpretation and Bibliography*. Metuchen, N.J.: Scarecrow Press.

Klein, Melanie. 1975. *Love, Guilt, and Reparation*. New York: Delacorte Press.

Kloppenborg, John S. 1988. *Q Parallels. Synopsis, Critical Notes, and Concordance*. Sonoma, Calif.: Polebridge Press.

_____. 1989. "The Dishonoured Master. Luke 16:1-8a." *Biblica* 4, 474-95.

Koester, Helmut. "Recovering the Original Meaning of Matthew's Parables." *Bible Review* 3 (June), 11, 52.

_____. 1992. "Finding Morality in Luke's Disturbing Parables." *Bible Review* 5 (October), 10.

Kohut, Heinz. 1977. *The Restoration of the Self*. New York: Charles Scribner's Sons.

Kojeve, Alexandre. 1969. *Introduction to the Reading of Hegel*. New York: Basic Books.

Kosinski, Jerzy. 1971. *Being There*. New York: Harcourt Press.

Lambrecht, Jan. 1983. *Once More Astonished. The Parables of Jesus*. New York: Crossroad.

_____. 1991. *Out of the Treasure. The Parables of the Gospel of Matthew*. Louvain Theological and Pastoral Monographs, 10. Louvain: Peeters Press. Grand Rapids, Mich.: Eerdmans.

Leavy, Stanley A. 1980. *The Psychoanalytic Dialogue*. New Haven: Yale University Press.

Lenski, Gerhard E. 1966. *Power and Privilege. A Theory of Social Stratification*. New York: McGraw Hill.

Linnemann, Eta. 1966. *Parables of Jesus. Introduction and Exposition*. Trans. John Sturdy. London: SPCK.

Mack, Burton L. 1988. *A Myth of Innocence. Mark and Christian Origins*. Philadelphia: Fortress.

_____. 1993. *The Lost Gospel. The Book of Q and Christian Origins*. San Francisco: HarperSanFrancisco.

_____. 1995. *Who Wrote the New Testament? The Making of the Christian Myth*. San Francisco: HarperSanFrancisco.

McGaughy, L. 1975. "The Fear of Yahweh and the Mission of Judaism: A Postexilic Maxim and Its Early Christian Expansion in the Parable of the Talents." *Journal of Biblical Literature* 94, 235-45.

Meier, John P. Vol. I: 1991; Vol. II: 1994. *A Marginal Jew. Rethinking the Historical Jesus*. New York: Doubleday.

Meshorer, Yaakov. 1979. "Sepphoris and Rome." In *Greek Numismatics and Archaeology. Essays in Honor of Margaret Thompson*. O. Morkholm and N. M. Waggoner, eds. Belgium: Cultura Press. 159-71.

Meyers, Eric M. "Roman Sepphoris in Light of New Archaeological Research." In *The Galilee in Late Antiquity*. Lee L. Levine, ed. New York: The Jewish Theological Seminary of America. Distributed by Harvard University Press, Cambridge, Mass. 321-38.

Michels, Robert. 1985. "Transference: An Introduction to the Concept." In *The Transference in Psychotherapy. Clinical Management*. Evelyne Albrecht Schwaber, ed. New York: International Universities Press. 13-19.

Milavec, Aaron A. 1989. "A Fresh Analysis of the Parable of the Wicked Husbandmen in the Light of Jewish-Catholic Dialogue." In *Parable and Story in Judaism and Christianity*. Clemens Thoma and Michael

Wyschogrod, eds. New York: Paulist Press. 81-117.

_____. 1990. "The Identity of 'the Son' and 'the Others.' Mark's Parable of The Wicked Husbandmen Reconsidered." *Biblical Theology Bulletin* 20: 30-37.

Miller, Alice. 1981. *The Drama of the Gifted Child.* New York: Basic Books.

Miller, Robert J., ed. 1994. *The Complete Gospels. Annotated Scholars' Version.* Revised and expanded. Sonoma, Calif.: Polebridge Press.

Mitchell, W. J. T., ed. 1980. *On Narrative.* Chicago: University of Chicago Press.

Muecke, Douglas C. 1982. *Irony and the Ironic.* Second Edition. London: Methuen.

Nonan, Albert. 1992. *Jesus Before Christianity.* Third Edition. Maryknoll, N.Y.: Orbis Books.

Nouwen, Henri J. M. 1992. *The Return of the Prodigal Son. A Meditation on Fathers, Brothers, and Sons.* New York: Doubleday.

Ngugi wa Thiong'o. 1987. *The Devil on the Cross.* Oxford, England: Heinemann.

Oakman, Douglas E. 1986. *Jesus and the Economic Questions of His Day.* Studies in the Bible and Early Christianity 8. Lewiston, New York and Queenstown, Ontario: Edwin Mellen Press.

_____. 1987. "The Buying Power of Two Denarii. A Comment on Luke 10:35." *Forum* 3, 4: 33-38.

Osofsky, Gilbert, comp. 1969. *Puttin' on Ole Massa. The Slave Narratives of Henry Bibb, William Wells Brown, and Solomon Northrup.* New York: Harper & Row.

Overman, J. Andrew. 1988. "Who Were the First Urban Christians? Urbanization in Galilee in the First Century." In *Society of Biblical Literature Seminar Papers* 1988. David J. Lull, ed. Society of Biblical Literature Seminar Papers 27. Atlanta: Scholars Press. 160-68.

Perrin, Norman. 1976. *Jesus and the Language of the Kingdom. Symbol and Metaphor in New Testament Interpretation.* Philadelphia: Fortress.

Perkins, Pheme. 1981. *Hearing the Parables of Jesus.* New York: Paulist Press.

Petersen, Norman R. 1985. *Rediscovering Paul. Philemon and the Sociology of Paul's Narrative World.* Philadelphia: Fortress.

Phillips, Adam. 1988. *Winnicott*. Cambridge, Mass.: Harvard University Press.

Plaut, W. Gunther. 1974. *Genesis. Vol. I of The Torah. A Modern Commentary*. New York: Union of American Hebrew Congregations.

Porter, Stanley E. 1990. "The Parable of the Unjust Steward (Luke 16:1-13): Irony Is the Key." In *The Bible in Three Dimensions. Essays in Celebration of Forty Years of Biblical Studies in the University of Sheffield*. David J. A. Clines, Stephen E. Fowl, and Stanley E. Porter, eds. Journal for the Study of the Old Testament Supplement Series 87. Sheffield, England: JSOT Press. 127-53.

_____. 1994. "Jesus and the Use of Greek in Galilee." In *Studying the Historical Jesus. Evaluations of the State of Current Research*. Bruce Chilton and Craig A. Evans, eds. Leiden, New York, Köln: E. J. Brill. 123-54.

Praeder, Susan Marie. "The Parable of the Judge and the Widow." Chapter 3 in *The Word in Women's Worlds. Four Parables*. Wilmington, Del.: Michael Glazier.

Raboteau, Albert J. 1978. *Slave Religion. The "Invisible Institution" in the Antebellum South*. New York: Oxford University Press.

Reed, Jonathan L. 1992. "Population Numbers, Urbanization, and Economics: Galilean Archaeology and the Historical Jesus." *Society of Biblical Literature Seminar Papers* 1994. Eugene H. Lovering, Jr., ed. Atlanta: Scholars Press. 203-19.

Roark, James L. 1977. *Masters Without Slaves. Southern Planters in the Civil War and Reconstruction*. New York: Norton.

Rohrbaugh, Richard L. 1993. "A Peasant Reading of the Parable of the Talents/Pounds: A Text of Terror?" *Biblical Theology Bulletin* 23:32-39.

Sanders, J. T. 1981. "The Parable of the Pounds and Lucan Anti-Semitism." *Theological Studies* 42: 660-68.

Sanford, John A. 1987. *The Kingdom Within: The Inner Meaning of Jesus' Sayings. Revised Edition*. San Francisco: HarperSanFrancisco.

Schafer, Roy. 1981. *Narrative Actions in Psychoanalysis*. Worcester, Mass.: Clark University Press.

_____. 1983. *The Analytic Attitude*. New York: Basic Books.

_____. 1997. "Conformity and Individualism." Chapter 2 in *The Inner World and the Outer World. Psychoanalytic Perspectives*. Edward R.

Shapiro, ed. New Haven, Conn.: Yale University Press.

Schneiders, Sandra M. 1991. *The Revelatory Text. Interpreting the New Testament as Sacred Scripture.* San Francisco: Harper.

_____. 1993. "Scripture as the Word of God." *Princeton Seminary Bulletin* 14, 1 (New Series): 18-35.

Scott, Bernard Brandon. 1989. *Hear Then the Parable. A Commentary on the Parables of Jesus.* Minneapolis: Fortress.

Senior, Donald. 1987. "Matthew 18:23-35." *Interpretation* 41: 403-07.

Shapiro, Edward R. and A Wesley Carr. 1991. *Lost in Familiar Places. Creating New Connections between the Individual and Society.* New Haven: Yale University Press.

Snodgrass, Klyne. 1983. *The Parable of the Wicked Tenants.* Tubingen: J. C. B. Mohr (Paul Siebeck).

Stern, David. 1991. *Parables in Midrash. Narrative and Exegesis in Rabbinic Literature.* Cambridge, Mass.: Harvard University Press.

Stolorow, Robert D. 1972. "On the Phenomenology of Anger and Hate." *The American Journal of Psychoanalysis* 32: 218-20.

Stroker, William D. 1988. "Extracanonical Parables and the Historical Jesus." *SEMEIA* 44: 95-120.

Tanakh: The Holy Scriptures. 1988. Philadelphia: The Jewish Publishing Society.

Telford, William R. 1994. "Major Trends and Interpretive Issues in the Study of Jesus." In *Studying the Historical Jesus. Evaluations of the State of Current Research.* Bruce Chilton and Craig A. Evans, eds. Leiden, New York, Köln: E. J. Brill. 33-74.

Thackeray, H. St. J., R. Marcus, A Eikgren, and L. H. Feldman, trans. 1926-1965. *Josephus.* 10 vols. Loeb Classical Library. Cambridge, Mass.: Harvard University Press.

Thurman, Howard. 1981 (1949). *Jesus and the Disinherited.* Richmond, Ind.: Friends United Press.

Tolbert, Mary Ann. 1997. "The Prodigal Son: An Essay in Literary Criticism from a Psychoanalytic Perspective." *SEMEIA* 9: 1–20

_____. 1979. *Perspectives on the Parables. An Approach to Multiple Interpretations.* Philadelphia: Fortress.

Topel, L. John. 1975. "On the Injustice of the Unjust Steward." *Catholic Biblical Quarterly* 37, 216-27.

Via, Dan O., Jr. 1967. *The Parables. Their Literary and Existential*

Dimension. Philadelphia: Fortress.

Von Rad, G. 1966. *The Problem of the Hexateuch and Other Essays.* Trans. E. W. T. Dicken. New York: McGraw-Hill.

Weaver, Walter P. and James H. Charlesworth, eds. 1995. *Earthing Christologies. From Jesus' Parables to Jesus the Parable.* Valley Forge, Pa.: Trinity Press International.

Westerman, Claus. 1990. *The Parables of Jesus in Light of the Old Testament.* Minneapolis: Fortress.

Winnicott, D.W. 1965. *The Maturational Processes and the Facilitating Environment.* New York: International Universities Press.

_____. 1975. Through Paediatrics to Psycho-Analysis. New York: Basic Books.

Yeivin, S. 1937. "Historical and Archaeological Notes." In *A Preliminary Report of the University of Michigan Excavation at Sepphoris, Palestine, in 1931.* Leroy Waterman, et al. Ann Arbor: University of Michigan Press. 17-34.

Young, Bradford H. 1989. *Jesus and His Jewish Parables.* New York: Paulist Press.

Zinner, J. 1976. "The Implications of Projective Identification for Marital Interaction." In *Contemporary Marriage. Structure, Dynamics and Therapy.* H. Grunebaum and J. Christ, eds. Boston: Little-Brown.

Index